The Copper Town Cookbook

Community Service Organization,
Copper Town Cookbook Committee
Haven United Methodist Church
of Jerome Presents:
The 18th Printing:
The Copper Town Cookbook

Eighteenth Printing

The Gallows Frame on our cover is located over the Edith Shaft on the Verde Exploration Limited Property. The cover and illustrations throughout were created and contributed by noted artist Frank M. Hamilton

Copyright 1972
Copper Town Cookbook
Haven United Methodist Church
Jerome, AZ

Manufactured by Friesens Corporation in Altona, Canada, November 2009, Job 50768

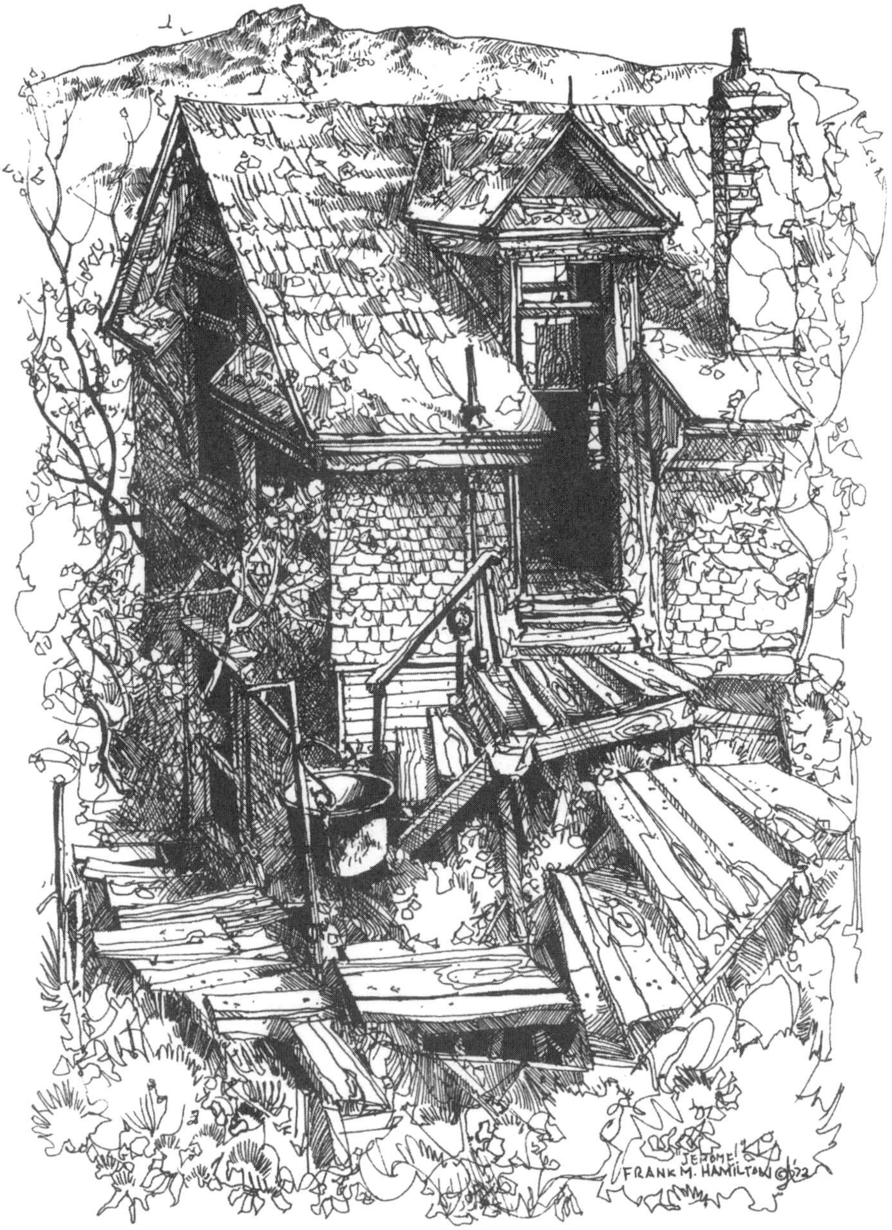
"JEROME!"
FRANK M. HAMILTON ©'72

CONTENTS

BREADS & ROLLS _____ 9

SALADS-DRESSINGS _____ 19

MEATS-CASSEROLES _____ 25

VEGETABLE DISHES _____ 43

MEXICAN DISHES _____ 53

CAKES & COOKIES _____ 63

DESSERTS & PASTRIES _____ 81

SPECIALTIES _____ 89

The original dedication page from 1972

Dear Friends — Old and New:

It has been with the greatest sense of pleasure and anticipation that we have worked together to compile our COPPER TOWN COOKBOOK.

We have attempted to give it something of the aura of a copper mining town and this decision has led us down a very interesting path. We have had responses from the east coast to the west coast, from oldtimers who think of Jerome with unwavering affection, from men as well as women who remember dishes concocted by dear ones, and who wish to share them with us. Some recipes, we are told, are typical of all mining towns and we are delighted to include them in our book.

Our present-day Jeromeites have been equally cooperative; they too have shown a willingness to share in a fund raising effort for the sole benefit of the town. In some cases, bits of information given us have been included because of their human interest value. We thank all of you for all you have contributed.

We are also deeply indebted to, and wish to express our gratitude to Rose Hiett, who, in spite of urgent demands upon her time, did all the IBM work for us. She also gave us the benefit of her wide knowledge of business acumen and labored faithfully to help produce an attractive and concisely worded book.

Another who deserves our appreciation for her patience and cooperation is Shirley Hamilton, wife of the artist, who assisted us on the art work and did the illustrations for the Mexican Dishes section of the book.

There are many others, too numerous to mention, who supported us and helped in many ways—layouts, typing, proofreading, correspondence, committee conferences and studies of cookbook techniques—besides all the donors of recipes. All this has been done by voluntary teamwork and we want everybody to know that we appreciate all your efforts.

November 1972   The Copper Town Cookbook Committee
                             Jerome, Arizona 86331

BREADS & ROLLS

WHOLE WHEAT BREAD

1-3/4 cups milk
2 teaspoons salt
1/3 cup olive oil
1/2 cup water

1/3 cup honey or sorghum
2 eggs
2 tablespoons active dry yeast
6 to 7 cups whole wheat flour

Scald milk and cool slightly; mix salt, oil, honey, water, eggs and yeast. Mix well. Sift flour and add to mixture enough to make dough the consistency of a cake; let stand 15 minutes. Sift and add more flour until too thick to stir with a spoon. Work with hands and then turn out on floured pastry cloth; fold and push; add flour, as needed; knead for 10 to 20 minutes until shiny. Put back into bowl and let rise until it is double in size, which takes about 45 minutes. Divide into two pieces and shape into loaves. Place in oven and set at 350° without preheating and bake for 1 hour. Brush top with butter or margarine while bread is still hot. This bread is delicious and nutritious.   Rose Hiett

FRENCH BREAD

1-1/4 cups warm water
1 tablespoon dry yeast
1-1/2 teaspoons salt
3 tablespoons soft shortening
4 cups flour, sifted

Measure warm water into large mixing bowl. Add dry yeast and stir until dissolved. Add salt, shortening and half the flour. Beat until smooth. Add enough of the remaining flour to handle easily. Turn the dough onto floured board, knead until smooth and elastic. Shape into a ball, place in greased bowl, cover and let rise until double in bulk. Punch down, pull edges into center and turn dough over in bowl. Cover and let rise again until almost double—about 30 minutes. Divide dough into two equal parts, each 15"x10"; roll up tightly, starting with wide side. Seal edges by pinching together. With a hand on each end, roll gently back and forth to lengthen loaf and taper ends. Place diagonally on a greased cookie sheet which has been sprinkled with corn meal. Make 1/4-inch deep slashes in top of loaf at 1-inch intervals. Brush top with cold water. Let stand uncovered until double in bulk—about 1 hour. Heat oven to 375° and when loaves have risen, brush tops again with cold water. Bake 45 minutes. Makes two loaves.

Johanna Blazina

ONION SHORTCAKE
(Men like this)

2 tablespoons butter
2-1/2 cups onions, thinly sliced
1/2 cup sour cream
2 eggs
Biscuit dough (scratch or mix)
Salt and pepper to taste

Melt butter in frying pan; add onions and cook until clear but not browned; season as desired. Roll out biscuit dough to 1/2 inch thickness and place in baking pan. Spread the onion over the top. Pour over all the sour cream which has been mixed with the beaten eggs. Bake as for ordinary biscuits in a hot oven for 12 to 15 minutes. Very good with roasts or steaks.

Jack Ward, Abilene, Texas

IRISH BREAD

4 cups flour
4 teaspoons baking powder
1 cup sugar
1/2 teaspoon salt
1 teaspoon caraway seeds, optional

1-1/2 cups raisins
2 eggs
1/2 cup margarine
1 cup milk

Sift flour, baking powder, sugar and salt together. Sprinkle a little over the raisins. Cut in margarine with pastry cutter. Add beaten eggs and milk and mix together. Turn onto floured board and mold into round loaf. Place in greased pan and bake 1 hour in 350° oven. Be careful not to over-bake.
                                                  Polly Warburton

CHEESE ROLL

1 large package cream cheese
5-ounce jar creamy blue cheese
5-ounce semi-soft English cheese

1/2 cup chopped onion (fine)
1/2 cup chopped nuts
Chopped parsley

Let cheese soften to room temperature. Blend cheese with the other ingredients. Chill overnight. Form into balls. Roll in nuts and then in parsley Use as appetizers.
                                                  Fay Horton

BRAN MUFFIN MIX

2 cups bran buds (cold cereal)
2 cups boiling water
2-1/2 cups sugar
1 cup oil
4 eggs

5 cups flour
5 teaspoons soda
1/2 teaspoon salt
4 cups All Bran
1 pound seedless raisins
1 quart buttermilk

Makes about 1 gallon batter which will keep several months in refrigerator to be used as needed for fresh hot muffins. Combine the boiling water with the bran buds and set aside. Cream together the sugar and oil; add the eggs one at a time, stirring well. Sift together the flour, soda and salt; add these sifted dry ingredients to the egg mixture alternately with the buttermilk. Mix thoroughly, then add the all-bran, the cooled bran buds and the raisins. Again mix thoroughly and store in tightly covered glass or plastic containers in non-freeze section of the refrigerator. Use as needed. Do not stir; scoop from bottom, if the raisins sink. Bake in muffin tins for 20 minutes at 400°.   Zella Davis

BUTTERHORNS

1 cup milk
1/2 cup sugar
1/2 cup shortening
3 eggs, beaten

1 teaspoon salt
4 cups flour, sifted
1 yeast cake

Melt sugar and shortening in warm milk. When cool add yeast cake. Allow to stand awhile after yeast has been added. Add eggs, flour and salt. Mix well and allow to rise. When light, divide into three portions. Roll out and cut in eight pieces like pie. Spread with brown sugar, butter and nuts. Roll each piece from outside to center so that the point of the wedge comes out on top. Place in shallow pan, close together or the goody will run out and butterhorns will be too dry). Allow to rise again. Bake at 350° for 30 to 40 minutes.   Fay Ivey
Clarkdale, AZ

BIDIE'S POTATO ROLLS

1 cake yeast, or 1 package dry yeast
1 cup mashed potatoes
1 cup sugar
3/4 cup shortening

4 eggs, slightly beaten
5-1/2 cups flour, or more, or less
1 teaspoon salt - to taste
1 cup lukewarm water

Soak yeast in 1 cup lukewarm water. Mash hot potatoes and stir in the sugar and the yeast and let rise in a warm place until bubbly, about 1 hour. Mix 1 cup of the flour with salt and beaten eggs; beat until smooth. Add enough remaining flour to make a soft dough; turn out on floured board and knead in about 1/2 cup flour. Don't let dough become too firm. Make out into rolls, place in greased pan and brush tops with melted butter. Let rise in warm place until double in bulk, about 2 hours. Bake at 375° for 15 to 20 minutes. Serve hot! (From the recipes of my Grandmother Bidie.)   Bertha May
Tucson, AZ

NUT BREAD

3 cups flour
1 cup granulated sugar
1 dessert spoonful of salt
3-1/4 teaspoons baking powder
1 cup walnuts, chopped

1 cup dates, chopped
1 cup sweet milk
2 eggs, well beaten
1 teaspoon vanilla

Sift together flour, sugar, salt and baking powder. Add walnuts and dates to flour mixture. Add milk and vanilla; stir well; lastly add eggs. Stir some more. Let stand in loaf pan for 20 minutes. Bake slowly for 1 hour at 300° and then finish the baking for another 30 minutes at 350° until nicely browned on top.   Muriel O'Boyle

MOM'S POVITIZA - AUSTRIAN NUT ROLL

2 cups milk
1 cube butter
1-1/2 cups sugar
4 eggs, well beaten

1 tablespoon salt
2 cakes yeast
7 cups flour
1 lemon, juice and rind

Scald together milk and butter; cool to lukewarm; combine with sugar, eggs, salt and yeast that has been dissolved in 1/4 cup warm water. Add 4 cups of the flour and beat smooth. Add juice and rind of lemon and mix well. Add 3 more cups flour to make dough easy to handle. Turn dough onto well floured board and knead 10 to 15 minutes or until soft, smooth and springy. Place in a well greased bowl; grease top of dough, cover and let rise until doubled in bulk; takes about 1 hour or until finger impression remains in dough. Roll out on well floured cloth into a large rectangle; roll at least 1/4-inch thin or thinner. Add nut filling (see recipe below), trim edges and save them for sweet bread. Roll jelly-roll style and place in well greased pan in swirl fashion. Cover and let rise in warm place, as follows: If more bread is desired, let rise 1 hour; if richer and less bread is desired, let rise for only 15 minutes. When ready to bake, brush top of dough gently with canned milk to brown nicely. Bake in 325° oven for 1 hour and 15 minutes. When done, turn right side on rack and let cool, uncovered.

NUT FILLING FOR MOM'S POVITIZA

1-1/2 pounds walnuts, ground
1-1/2 cups sugar
2 teaspoons cinnamon
1/2 teaspoon allspice

1/4 teaspoon cloves
1/2 teaspoon salt
4 eggs, well beaten
1 large can milk

Combine all the above and mix thoroughly. Set aside in warm place until needed. If too thick, thin out with more milk to the consistency necessary for easy spreading on the dough.

Joan Radetich Cirata, Palm Springs, California

QUICK ROLLS

1 cake compressed yeast, or 1 package active yeast granules
2/3 cup warm milk
2 cups Bisquick
Butter, as needed

Dissolve yeast in milk; add Bisquick and knead well. Roll out to 1/2-inch thick. Cut with biscuit cutter; spread with butter; turn over in pan. Let rise 15 to 25 minutes in hot oven 400° and serve hot.

Mattie Leyel

POVITISA-YUGOSLAVIAN HOLIDAY BREAD

2 small yeast cakes
3 teaspoons sugar
1 teaspoon salt
1 cup water, lukewarm

1 cup shortening, melted
1 cup sugar
8 eggs, well beaten
8 cups all-purpose flour

Dissolve yeast cakes in mixture of 3 teaspoons sugar, the salt and lukewarm water. Next add the rest of the sugar to the melted shortening and the eggs. Then add the yeast mixture which has begun to bubble. The sifted flour is then added gradually. When the dough becomes stiff, knead for about 5 minutes. Let dough rise until double its original size; this takes about 1-1/2 hours. Roll the dough out on an extra large dish towel stretched out on the kitchen table. The towel must be floured and dough rolled out to 1/4-inch thickness in a circle about 3 feet in diameter. (I have changed this; divide dough into 4 equal parts; it is much easier to handle.)

FILLING FOR POVITISA:

1/2 pound butter
3 or 4 large cans walnuts, ground
1/2 cup granulated sugar

1/4 cup brown sugar
1 egg
1-1/2 teaspoon cinnamon
1 teaspoon allspice

Mix all ingredients together. Spread filling on dough and sprinkle with raisins. Crimp to prevent filling from spilling over sides. Now take two adjacent corners of the towel and flip, rolling the dough as in a jelly roll. Place gently in 9-inch cake pans lined with floured brown paper. Curve rolled dough in the shape of a ring. Let rise about 2 hours. Bake in 325° oven for 45 minutes to 1 hour. This pastry is very popular; always in demand for our bake sales.

Margaret Cambruzzi

LEMON BREAD

1/2 cup shortening
1-1/2 cups sugar (includes topping)
2 eggs, beaten
1/2 cup milk

1 lemon, grated
1-1/2 cups flour
1 teaspoon baking powder
1/2 teaspoon salt
1/2 teaspoon lemon flavoring

Cream shortening and 1 cup sugar. Add eggs, then milk alternately with baking powder and salt that have been sifted with flour. Add grated lemon and flavoring to mixture. Bake in loaf pan 45 minutes in 350° oven. After it is baked and still warm, pour juice of lemon mixed with 1/2 cup of sugar over the bread.

Ellen Vojnic

CINNAMON BUNS

2 cakes Fleischmann's yeast
1 tablespoon sugar
1 cup lukewarm water
1 cup milk
3 eggs, beaten

6 tablespoons shortening
1/2 cup sugar
1 teaspoon salt
7 cups sifted flour

Dissolve yeast and 1 tablespoon of sugar in lukewarm water; scald the milk; add shortening, rest of sugar and salt; cool to lukewarm; add 2 cups of the flour to make a batter. Add yeast and beaten eggs; beat well. Add remaining flour or enough to make a soft dough. Knead it lightly and place in greased bowl. Cover and set in warm place free from draft. Let rise until doubled in bulk, about 2 hours. When light, punch down the dough and shape into ball. (See filling recipe below.)

FILLING FOR CINNAMON BUNS

1 cube butter, or margarine, melted
1 tablespoon cinnamon

1-1/2 cups brown sugar
1 cup raisins
1 cup nuts, ground

When dough is light and punched down, divide into 2 equal portions. Roll out into oblong pieces 1/4-inch thick. Brush with melted butter or margarine and sprinkle with brown sugar, cinnamon, raisins and nuts. Roll up as for jelly rolls and cut in 1-inch slices. Place cut side up about 1 inch apart in a large shallow greased baking pan. Cover and let rise in warm place free from draft until light; about 1 hour. Bake in hot oven at 425° about 20 minutes. Ice the tops of buns while they are still warm. (See icing recipe below)

ICING FOR CINNAMON BUNS

4 teaspoons milk, or warm water
1/2 teaspoon vanilla

1 cup confectioners' sugar, sifted

Add milk or water slowly to sugar to make a smooth, fairly thick paste. Add extract. Water will make a more transparent icing than milk.

Ann Radetich Kauzlaric, Gallup, New Mexico

❖ ❖ ❖ ❖ ❖ ❖ ❖

"The Town of Jerome sits on 88 miles of old copper mine tunnels."

RUM BABAS (MUFFINS)

1 package dry yeast	1/8 pound butter
1/3 cup warm water or milk, or more	1/4 cup currants
2 eggs	1/4 cup raisins, white
2 cups flour	1/4 cup candied fruit

Dissolve yeast in water or milk; add eggs, 1 cup of the flour, the butter and salt. Stir and beat thoroughly. Let this sponge stand at 80 or 85° till double, which takes about 1 hour. Bake at 375° about 35 minutes. Remove from oven and place in square pan and pour the syrup (Recipe below) over the muffins. Turn muffins over once in awhile. This is served like a pudding and should be warm.

Syrup:
1 large can (1 quart and 14 ounces) apricot nectar
2 cups sugar
Juice of 1 large lemon
2 tablespoons rum flavor
2 wine glasses of heavy rum

Boil apricot nectar and sugar for 10 to 12 minutes. Add lemon juice and remove from stove. Add rum flavoring and heavy rum. Save about 1/3 of the syrup and at serving time it can be reheated and added.

Myrtle Boyd

PORTZILKE — RAISIN FRITTERS
(Pronounced Port'-sill-cha) Low German; Porzelchen, High German

2 cups milk	1-1/2 teaspoon salt
1/4 cup butter	2 cups raisins
3 eggs	1 cake yeast
1/2 cup sugar	4 cups flour

These raisin fritters were made especially for New Year's Day. The name means "tumbling over" since they turn over by themselves when they are dropped into the deep fat. First scald the milk; cool to lukewarm and dissolve yeast in lukewarm milk. Add remaining ingredients. Mix well; let rise until double in bulk. Drop into deep fat by spoonfuls and fry until brown. (An assist in turning the Portzilke usually is necessary, despite the "tumbling over" name!)

Kathryn J. Mathews

PUMPKIN BREAD

3 cups sugar
1 cup oil
4 eggs
2 cups pumpkin
2/3 cup water
3-1/2 cups flour
2 teaspoons soda

1/2 teaspoon baking powder
1-1/2 teaspoons salt
1 teaspoon cinnamon
1/2 teaspoon cloves
1/2 cup nuts, chopped
1 cup dates or raisins, chopped

Mix ingredients and pour into four 1-pound greased coffee cans until cans are half full. Bake at 350° for 1 hour.

Zella Davis

FRIED INDIAN BREAD

4 cups unsifted flour
1 teaspoon salt
3 teaspoons baking powder
1-1/4 cups lukewarm water

Mix dry ingredients. Add water and knead thoroughly. Cover and let stand 10 minutes. Roll dough into balls about 2 inches in diameter and roll them out flat with a rolling pin. Cut two slashes in center. Fry on both sides in hot grease until brown. Makes 10 to 12 portions.

Ethel Devine

BANANA BREAD

3 medium size bananas, mashed
1/2 cup shortening
1 cup sugar
2 eggs
2 cups sifted flour

1 teaspoon soda
1/2 teaspoon baking powder
1/2 teaspoon salt
Nuts, if desired

Cream shortening and sugar; add eggs, then dry ingredients. Alternate with banana mixture. Bake in loaf pan 350° oven for 40 to 45 minutes.

Ethel Devine

DUTCH DILL BREAD

2 cups potato water
1/2 cup sugar
1-1/2 teaspoon salt
2 cakes, or 2 packages, yeast
1 egg
1/4 cup soft shortening
6 to 7 cups flour
4 tablespoons dill seed

Have the flour measured and ready in large bowl for the liquid mixture. Dissolve yeast in the lukewarm potato water, sugar and salt; stir well and add the egg and soft shortening. Knead all until a smooth gloss is obtained in the dough. This takes at least 10 minutes of kneading. Form into loaves or rolls; spread tops with thin coat of grease. Pat dill seeds on gently. Cover with wet towel and place in warm area to rise. If preferred, add the dill seed in with the flour at mixing time; this will give the bread a truer dill flavor. This bread can be used immediately, or it may be stored in the refrigerator and baked at a later time, but the recommended time for such storage should not exceed 2 weeks and the dough should be stored in an air-tight container.

Esther Meusch

SALADS — DRESSINGS

CRANBERRY SALAD

1 quart raw cranberries
3 red apples
1 orange
1 package cherry jello
2 cups sugar

Grind berries, apples with skins, orange with 1/2 of its peeling. Add sugar; let stand 24 hours. Make the jello by its own recipe and cool the liquid before adding the cranberry mixture. (This is a recipe from my Mary's cookbook.)   Val Harris, Berkeley, California

INDIAN SUMMER SALAD

1 large package orange jello
2 cups boiling water
1 cup frozen orange juice
1 can (No. 2) crushed
    pineapple, undrained
1 cup mandarin oranges,
    drained
1 package Dream Whip
1 package prepared
    lemon pudding

Dissolve jello in water; add juice and fruit. When firm, top with Dream Whip mixed with lemon pudding.
              Ethel Devine, Bishop, California

BEAN SALAD

1 can French style green beans, drained
1 can extra small peas
3 stalks celery, cut up
1 small onion, cut up
1 mango, cut up
1 small can pimentos

Accent as desired
1-1/2 cup sugar
1 cup vinegar
Paprika to taste
1 tablespoon salt
1 tablespoon water

Mix sugar, Accent, vinegar, paprika, salt and water until sugar is dissolved. Then combine with the rest of the ingredients and let the salad mixture set in refrigerator 24 hours. Drain when you serve. Will keep in refrigerator indefinitely.

Clyne Murray

HOLIDAY SALAD

2 packages small (or 1 large) raspberry Jello
1 cup boiling water
1 cup Port wine
1 can whole cranberry sauce
1 can crushed pineapple
2 tablespoons lemon juice
Nuts (optional)

Serve with sour cream.

Winifred S. Foster

RECEPTION SALAD PAR EXCELLENT

1 package lemon Jello
1 large can of crushed pineapple
1 small can pimento
1 large package Philadelphia cream cheese
2/3 cup nutmeats, chopped
1/2 cup celery, diced
1/2 pint whipping cream

Dissolve the jello in the juice of the can of crushed pineapple which has been boiled. When cool add the pimento which has been creamed with the Philadelphia cream cheese, the celery, chopped nutmeats and the crushed pineapple pulp. Lastly add the whipped cream and let set until mixture is firm and ready to be served.

Gladys Crow

GERMAN CABBAGE SALAD

1 large head of cabbage, shredded fine
1 medium size onion, minced
3/4 cup sugar
3/4 cup salad oil

Dressing ingredients:
1 cup vinegar
1 tablespoon sugar
1-1/2 teaspoons salt
1 teaspoon celery seed
1 teaspoon dry mustard

Prepare cabbage and onion; cover with the sugar and set aside to blend. Combine dressing ingredients and bring to a boil; add salad oil and bring to a boil again; pour dressing mixture over the cabbage mixture. Cover and let cool to room temperature. Refrigerate for at least 12 hours.

Lynn Rose

APPLE SAUCE SALAD

1/3 cup red hot candies
1 cup hot water
1/2 teaspoon salt
1 small can crushed pineapple

Pinch of nutmeg
2 teaspoons lemon juice
1 package lemon jello
1 can apple sauce

Follow directions for the jello. Add other ingredients. Pour into molds or rectangular pan and refrigerate. Let set in refrigerator at least 1 hour.

Grace Moore

FROZEN LIME BUTTERMINT SALAD

2 tall cans (13-1/2 ounce cans) crushed pineapple; don't drain
1 package (3 ounce size) lime jello (do not dissolve)
1 package (10 ounce size) miniature marshmallows
1 package (7 ounce size) Kraft Buttermints, crushed
1 pint whipping cream, whipped; or 2 packages prepared topping

Pour pineapple into large bowl; add jello powder and marshmallows. Mix well; cover bowl and set in refrigerator overnight. In the morning whip the cream or other topping and fold in crushed buttermints. Mix all ingredients together. Pour into 9"x13" cake pan and freeze. Remove from freezer 10 minutes before serving. Cut in squares and serve on lettuce leaf.

Sandra Smull Holiday

GOLDEN FRUIT FREEZE

1 can (11-ounce) mandarin orange sections, drained and halved
1 can (8-3/4-ounce) crushed pineapple (drained, 3/4 cup)
1/4 cup sugar
1 cup small curd cream style cottage cheese
1 package (2-ounce) dessert topping (dream whip)
1/2 cup milk
1 teaspoon vanilla
1/3 cup mayonnaise, or salad dressing

Combine fruits and sugar; mix well. In mixer bowl combine cottage cheese, dessert topping mix; add milk and vanilla. Beat smooth with rotary or electric mixer. Fold in fruit and mayonnaise. Turn into 8x8x2-inch pan. Freeze. To serve, let stand at room temperature for 15 minutes. Cut into squares. Makes 6 to 8 servings.

Mary Smull Cole
Independence, OR

COLD PEA SALAD

1 can (No. 303) sweet green peas, drained
5 or 6 hard boiled eggs, chopped fine
1 onion, chopped fine
1 small bell pepper, chopped fine
6 stalks celery, chopped fine
1/2 hunk cheddar cheese, diced fine

Mix ingredients, adding spices and mayonnaise, or salad dressing, to taste and blend well.
Martha Sharp

STRAWBERRY SALAD

2 packages strawberry gelatin   1 carton sour cream
2 cups boiling water
1 large package frozen strawberries
1 small can crushed pineapple

Dissolve gelatin in boiling water. Add thawed strawberries with juice from undrained pineapple. Pour 1/2 of the mixture into 8x12-inch baking dish and chill until set. Keep remaining gelatin at room temperature. Spread carton of dairy cream over top of congealed layer. Cover with remaining gelatin and chill until firm.
Ruth Kruse

THREE BEAN SALAD

1 can cut green beans
1 can cut wax beans
1 can red kidney beans
1 medium onion, chopped
3/4 cup sugar

1 teaspoon salt
1/2 teaspoon pepper
1/2 cup salad oil
2/3 cup vinegar

Rinse the juice off the beans thoroughly. Mix everything and marinate for 24 hours. Before serving drain all the dressing off and pour beans into lettuce-lined bowl. Myrel McDonald Alenius, Phoenix, Arizona

CRANBERRY SHERBET

1 pound cranberries
1/2 cup boiling water
1 teaspoon gelatin

1/4 cup cold water
2 cups sugar
1 pint ginger ale

Cook together cranberries and boiling water. Strain. Soak gelatin in cold water, add sugar and ginger ale. Chill in freezing tray; before it gets stiff, beat well. Makes 1 tray and may be frozen in icecream freezer.

Olga Berg

LIME AND COTTAGE CHEESE SALAD

1 package lime jello
1 can (No. 303) crushed pineapple,
   do not drain

1 cup cottage cheese
1 small carton cool whip
Maraschino cherries, nuts

Mix jello and pineapple together and bring to a boil. Cool and refrigerate until mixture starts to thicken. Fold in 1 cup cottage cheese and then fold in the cool whip. Return to refrigerator; when completely set, decorate with cherries and nuts, as preferred.

Beverly Sullivan

❖ ❖ ❖ ❖ ❖ ❖ ❖

"In 1904, in Jerome, there was a complaint because meat prices were too high. It was disgraceful, so housewives said: Porterhouse steak, 25 cents a pound, sirloin, 20 cents---."

FIVE CUP FRUIT SALAD

1 cup chunk pineapple, drained
1 cup canned mandarin oranges, drained
1 cup coconut, shredded
1 cup miniature marshmallows
1 cup sour cream

Mix well and chill. May be made the day before serving.

Anna Cram

RUSSIAN SALAD DRESSING

3/4 cup sugar
1 cup vinegar
1 cup oil
1 teaspoon paprika
1/2 teaspoon celery salt

1 teaspoon salt
1 medium onion, grated
1 green pepper, diced
2/3 cup catsup
2 teaspoons dry mustard
1 clove garlic

Beat vinegar into oil; add sugar and mix in remaining ingredients. Shake well before using.

Margaret Smull

TOMATO FRENCH DRESSING

1-1/2 cups salad oil
1 can tomato soup (Heinz condensed) undiluted
1 cup Heinz vinegar
1/2 cup water
1/3 cup sugar
1 tablespoon Worcestershire sauce
1 teaspoon salt
1 teaspoon minced onion
1 teaspoon mild mustard
1/2 teaspoon paprika
1/2 teaspoon pepper

Combine ingredients; beat with rotary beater; chill; stir before serving. Makes 1 quart.

Gladys Crow

MEATS × CASSEROLES

OVEN BARBECUED POT ROAST

3 to 4 pound pot roast (chuck roast)
Flour to dust the roast
    Barbecue Sauce:
1 tablespoon Worchestershire sauce
1 clove garlic
Dash of thyme, basil and oregano
1/2 cup red wine.

Place in heavy pan or Dutch oven. Pour over it the remaining ingredients made into a sauce. Cover and bake in slow oven 325° for 2-1/2 hours, or until tender. Serve the roast with green beans dressed with toasted sliced almonds; fruit salad, lemon pie and coffee.

                                                                  Jane Troyer

MOM'S SAUERKRAUT WITH POLISH SAUSAGES

1 can (No. 2-1/2) sauerkraut
1 can (16-ounce) pork and beans
1 can tomato soup
1 can tomato sauce

1 clove garlic, minced
5 slices bacon, diced
6 Polish sausages, cut
    to serving size

Place all ingredients in a large pot. Add enough water to make it soupy, but not thin. Bring to a simmer and cook for 1-1/2 hours. Serve with French bread.
                                                    Joan Radetich Cirata

CORNISH PASTY

1 pound tender steak, round or sirloin
3 medium size potatoes
1 large onion
1/2 cube of butter

4 cups of flour
1 cup Crisco
5 to 6 tablespoons
ice water
Salt and pepper

Cut the steak and potatoes into small pieces. Chop the onions until fine. Set these three ingredients aside. Mix Crisco in flour and salt a little at a time. Gradually add water until dough is mealy. Roll out the dough into 4 portions, so that each portion is the size of a dinner plate. Butter the crust, leaving 2 inches to the edge. Add the ingredients—equal portions on each piece of dough—placing the meat on the bottom and sprinkling the chopped onions on the top. Place a piece of butter, and salt and pepper to taste, on the top of the ingredients. Roll each crust over like a dumpling; crimp the edges and slit the top. Bake at 350° for 1 hour. This recipe by former Jerome resident Madge Whitford Smith of Glendale, Arizona, is sent in to you by her son, Douglas P. Whitford of Glendale and also by Madge's nephew, Robert B. Ross, also former Jeromeites. Madge made these pasties for her husband Fred Whitford, Doug's father, to take to work at Little Daisy mine. Fred brought the recipe from his native Cornwall, England.

Robert Baldwin Ross

COPPER COUNTRY PASTY RECIPE

3 cups flour
3/4 cup lard or other shortening
1 teaspoon salt
2/3 cup cold water

FILLING:
1 pound flank or round steak, diced
1/2 pound pork, diced
Potatoes, finely chopped
Salt and pepper to taste
Turnips, or rutabagas
Onion, sliced
Butter, as desired

Mix flour, shortening, salt and add enough water to make dough just a little more moist than pastry dough. Divide in 4 parts. Roll each piece into the size of a dinner plate. On half of each piece of rolled dough cover as follows with the filling ingredients: 1/2-inch layer of potatoes; season these with salt and pepper. Follow with a thin layer of turnips or rutabagas, then a thin layer of onions. Next cover with 1/4 of the beef and pork mixed and seasoned. Add butter the size of a walnut on top. Then fold the uncovered portion of dough over the filled portion. Crimp the edges. Pasty is somewhat in shape of halfmoon. Make 1-inch slit on top of dough. Bake on cookie sheet or pie pan at 400° for 1 hour. Recipe makes 4 pasties.

Irma Killough

MEAT LOAF

1-1/2 pounds ground beef
1 cup medium cracker crumbs
2 eggs, beaten
1/2 cup onions, chopped
2 tablespoons green pepper, chopped
Chili sauce, as needed

1/2 teaspoon salt
Dash thyme
Dash marjoram
2 tablespoons horseradish
4 teaspoons Worcestershire sauce

Combine all ingredients, except chili sauce. Mix well and shape this mixture into a loaf in a baking dish. Score the loaf by pressing top with wooden handle of spoon. Fill the score marks with chili sauce. Stick a bay leaf in the meat loaf and bake in 350° oven for 1 hour.

Sally Mongini

SHORT RIBS BURGUNDY

3 pounds short ribs cut 2 to 3 inches long
OR 3 pounds country-style spare ribs
3 tablespoons fat
1 medium size onion, chopped
1 tablespoon worcestershire sauce
1 teaspoon dry mustard
1/2 cup celery, diced

2 teaspoons salt
1/4 cup vinegar
2 tablespoons brown sugar
1/2 cup tomato catsup
1/2 cup burgundy, or other red table wine

Trim excess fat off meat. Brown ribs in hot fat. Then drain off all fat. Add other ingredients. Cover and cook slowly or bake at 350° for 1-1/2 hours. Serves 4 or 5 generously.

Ruth Kruse

PORK CHOPS BAKED IN SOUR CREAM

4 loin pork chops
Flour, or bread crumbs, as needed
Seasoning, as desired
4 whole cloves
Lard or pork drippings, as needed
1/2 bay leaf

1/2 cup water, or meat stock
2 tablespoons vinegar, or less, if preferred
1 tablespoon sugar
1/2 cup sour cream

Pre-heat oven to 350°. Dredge pork chops with seasoned flour or bread crumbs. Insert in each chop one clove. Brown lightly in little fat and place in baking dish. Combine remaining ingredients and pour over the chops. Bake covered about 1 hour. "Yummy!"

Mrs. Charles M. Coppedge

MEATBALL PAPRIKASH

2 cups soft bread crumbs, about 3 slices
1 pound lean ground beef
8 ounces prepared pork sausage
2 packages (6-ounce size) long grain and wild rice mix
1/4 cup all-purpose flour
1-3/4 cups water
1/4 teaspoon dried thyme, crushed
1/4 teaspoon celery seed
2 teaspoons paprika

3 eggs, beaten
1/2 cup milk
1 teaspoon paprika
1 teaspoon salt
1 teaspoon dry mustard
3/4 cup beef broth
1 tablespoon catsup
1 cup sour cream
1/8 teaspoon pepper

Combine bread crumbs, eggs, milk, paprika, salt, mustard, thyme, celery seed and pepper. Add ground beef and pork sausage and mix thoroughly. Shape into 40 small meatballs. Place in shallow baking pan and bake in 350° oven for 30 minutes. Drain and set aside. Meanwhile, cook rice mixes according to package directions. Stir together flour, water, beef broth and catsup; cook and stir until thickened. Stir in sour cream. Stir about half the sauce into the rice, and then turn this rice mixture into a baking dish 1-3/4 x 13-1/2 x 8-3/4 inches. Arrange the meatballs atop the rice, and pour on the remaining sour cream sauce. Bake uncovered in 350° oven for 30 to 35 minutes longer, or until the mixture is heated through. Serves 8 people.

Frank Eberdt

AUSTRALIAN PEPPER STEAK

2 pounds round steak
2 cups onions, chopped
2 garlic cloves, crushed
2 tablespoons olive oil
2 tablespoons butter, melted
1 teaspoon salt
1/2 teaspoon celery salt

1/4 teaspoon pepper
3-1/3 cups Italian pear-shaped tomatoes
1 cube beef bouillon
1 green pepper, sliced
2 tablespoons cornstarch
2 tablespoons Worchester sauce

Have steak tenderized. Trim fat from steak. Cut into strips about 2 inches wide. Brown meat, onions and garlic in butter and oil in large skillet. Add salt, celery salt, pepper, tomatoes, bouillon cube and green pepper. Cover and simmer 30 to 45 minutes, or until meat is tender. Combine cornstarch and Worchestershire sauce. Stir into meat mixture. Cook until thickened. Serve with mashed potatoes, cooked rice or noodles. Serves 6 people.

Olga Svob Dugan, Downey, California

HOLLAND CROQUETTES—also COCKTAIL CROQUETTES

3 tablespoons flour to each 1 cup of liquid, as needed for white sauce
Milk, bouillon, or water, as desired for liquid choice in the sauce
Salt and pepper to taste   Deep fat for cooking
Beef, veal, pork, chicken or seafood—as desired for meat choice
Celery or celery leaves, minced   2 eggs
Bread crumbs, as needed   4 tablespoons water

This recipe cannot be made in one day, since the mixture of which the croquettes are formed must stiffen overnight in the refrigerator. They can be made with either cooked beef, veal, pork, chicken, or seafood.

Make an extra thick white sauce, using at least 3 tablespoons of flour to each cup of liquid. The liquid should be milk for seafood croquettes and can be either water or bouillon for the others. Add minced celery or preferably celery leaves and minced onion. Finish sauce with salt and pepper. If cocktail croquettes are planned, season more highly. After sauce is finished, stir in minced meat or seafood. It is better to cut this than grind it, though grinding is possible. After bringing it to a boil, pour the sauce into rectangular cake pan, spreading it about 3/4-inch thick. Cover with plastic wrap; place in refrigerator. The stiffer this mix is, the easier to shape in croquettes.

NEXT DAY remove plastic covering. Turn contents out on a layer of bread crumbs to prevent sticking. With a long sharp knife cut into strips about 3/4-inch wide. (Be sure to clean knife after each cut.) For croquettes cut the strips into less than 2-inch lengths. Now roll each piece in breadcrumbs to prevent sticking and roll and shape without touching with the hands until covered with the crumbs. When they are all covered, beat two eggs with 4 tablespoons of cold water just enough to be well mixed. Now pick up croquette and moisten the short ends with the egg mixture, then roll them into it. Lift them out with a spatula or very wide fork (a normal fork will cause them to break) and toss them into a layer of bread crumbs. Cover with more crumbs and now roll them into final shape, making sure that there are no spots where the crumbs did not adhere. Let them dry for about 1 hour before frying in deep fat at 350° to drain on absorbent paper. The cocktail croquettes being balls are easier to form, but the operation is the same. These croquettes make an excellent luncheon dish, even more so since they can be fried at the last minute; the frying takes but 2 minutes.

                                                                                  John Figi

BEEF BOURGUIGNOUNE

2 pounds of lean tender beef,
   cut in 1-1/2 inch cubes
1-1/2 teaspoons salt
1/4 teaspoon pepper
2 tablespoons cooking oil
1 onion, coarsely chopped
1 carrot, coarsely chopped
1 stalk celery, coarsely chopped
1 can (No. 10-1/2) beef broth
1/2 cup red table wine
1/2 cup tomato puree
1/4 teaspoon thyme
1 small bay leaf
2 tablespoons butter
3 tablespoons flour
Mushrooms, as desired
Tiny boiled onions,
   as desired

Sprinkle meat with salt and pepper and brown in oil in Dutch oven. Remove beef and add vegetables and brown lightly. Return meat to Dutch oven. Add broth, wine, tomato puree, thyme and bay leaf. Cover tightly and bake in moderate 350° oven about 2 hours, or until beef is tender. Lift out the beef and keep it warm. To remaining liquid add flour browned in butter. Cook and stir until thickened; pour over beef. Garnish with 1/2 pound cooked fresh mushrooms and tiny boiled onions.

                                            Dorothy King Goss

CHUCK WAGON MARINADE
(For Crushed Pepper Steak below)

2 tablespoons instant onion flakes
2 teaspoons thyme
1 teaspoon marjoram
1 bay leaf, crushed
1 cup wine vinegar
1/2 cup oil
3 tablespoons lemon juice

CRUSHED PEPPER BARBECUED STEAK

Meat, your choice and amount needed, marinaded
1 cup peppercorns

Marinade meat in sauce for at least 1/2 day. Crush the peppercorns and with wooden mallet pound them into steak. Barbecue as usual, being careful not to lose the pepper in the process.

                                            Dorothy King Goss

ROLADA (MEAT AND VEGETABLE DISH)

1 full round of steak
1 medium size onion
1 piece of celery
1 clove of garlic
3 or 4 pieces of lunchmeat of your choice
Small handful of fresh parsley
Butter or margarine, as preferred
Salt and pepper to taste

Have your butcher run the steak through the tenderizer. Put onions, celery, garlic, lunchmeat and parsley through your food chopper. Then spread this mixture on the steak. Roll up as for a jelly roll. Place in cooking pan with the butter or margarine. Cover and bake at 350° for 1 hour. Makes a lot of juice, which can be used to make gravy. This is a "super" favorite when sliced cold and served in sandwiches.

Mary Beneitone

GREEN CHILI PORK ROAST

3 to 4 pound pork roast
1 large onion
2 large cloves garlic
4 large fresh green chilies (after removing some of the seeds)
3 large fresh tomatoes
Salt and pepper to taste

Brown meat. Add other ingredients. Simmer slowly for 4 hours. Salt and pepper to taste.

Frankie Vincent

PORCUPINES

1 pound ground beef (shaped into balls)
1/2 teaspoon salt
1/4 cup washed, uncooked rice
1 small onion chopped
1/8 teaspoon pepper

1 quart tomatoes
1 small bay leaf

In large skillet combine and bring to boil the tomatoes, sliced onion, salt, pepper and bay leaf (crushed). Place meat balls in frying pan. Simmer, turning occasionally for 45 min. Serve with sauce.

Hazel Statzell

CORNISH PASTIES (MEAT AND VEGETABLE DISH)

Pastry Recipe:
2 cups flour
1/2 cup lard, or vegetable shortening
1 cup beef suet, finely chopped or put through fine blade of a food chopper
3/4 teaspoon salt
4 to 6 tablespoons ice water

Filling Recipe:
2 pounds round steak or other lean beef cut in 1/2" cubes
2 to 3 medium potatoes, peeled and cubed
2 to 3 small onions, peeled and cubed
Salt and pepper to taste

These hearty Pasties (pronounced PAST-ease) were great favorites with the early pioneers. First, prepare the dough using the pastry recipe. Blend flour, salt and shortening with the finger tips until the mixture resembles cornmeal. Add the chopped suet and toss with a fork until mixed thoroughly. Add the water, using only enough to hold the dough together. Knead very lightly. Form into a ball and refrigerate an hour or so before rolling the dough. Next prepare the filling recipe by combining the meat, potatoes, onions and seasoning, tossing the mixture thoroughly. Finally, roll out portions of the dough on a floured board, bearing down somewhat heavily to flatten the pieces of suet in the dough into circles 8 to 9 inches in diameter. Cover half of a circle with the meat filling. Dot with butter. Moisten half the circumference with water, fold the empty side of the circle over, and seal the edges with the fingers or tines of a fork. Continue making the pasties until all of the ingredients are used. Bake the pasties on a cookie sheet at 350° for 1 hour. "There are probably as many recipes for pasties as there are people who have made them, but I never think of Jerome without remembering these Cornish Pasties." Submitted from the kitchen of Poppa Rice and Aunt Kate of Jerome from 1919 to 1927.

Leonard Connor, Milford, Pa.

BEEF STROGANOFF

1/2 pound large mushrooms, sliced
2 onions, sliced thin
1 pound round steak
1 teaspoon salt
1/2 teaspoon pepper

1 teaspoon sweet basil
1 clove garlic, pressed
1-1/4 cups sherry
1 pint sour cream
Safflower oil as needed

Cut meat into 1/2 x 6-inch strips. Put in mixing bowl. Mix meat and seasonings; add enough oil to moisten and knead by hand. Saute onions and mushrooms in safflower oil. Braise meat. Mix meat with onions and mushrooms in Dutch oven; cover with sherry and bring to a boil. Cook at low temperature for about 1 hour. Add sour cream and cook until the sour cream has a brownish color.

Lynn Rose

SWEDISH MEAT BALLS IN BURGUNDY

3/4 pound ground round, or chuck
3/4 cup bread crumbs or cornflake crumbs
1 small onion, minced
3/4 teaspoon cornstarch
Dash of allspice
1 egg, beaten
3/4 cup light cream
1-1/2 teaspoon salt

1/4 cup salad oil
3 tablespoons flour
2 cups water
1 cup burgundy
2 beef bouillon cubes
1/8 teaspoon pepper
1-1/2 teaspoon sugar
Bottled sauce for gravy

Combine chuck, crumbs, onion, cornstarch, allspice, egg, cream and 3/4 teaspoon of the salt. Shape into balls. Then heat fat in skillet and brown the balls on all sides and transfer them to dish. Next stir into fat the flour, water, burgundy, bouillon cubes, salt, pepper, sugar and bottled sauce to make a brown gravy (optional). Stir till smooth. Arrange meat balls in sauce. Simmer covered for 30 minutes. If desired, put balls and sauce in casserole and cook in oven. (Recipe from teacher at Jerome High School 1924-27 who lived in Jerome until 1932.

Winnie Vedder Bersinger
Bishop, California

CURRY STEAK

1 pound round steak
Seasoned flour, as needed
1 onion, sliced
1 teaspoon curry powder
2 tablespoons vinegar
4 tablespoons ketchup

1 cup hot stock, or make bouillon with 2 cubes per cup of hot water
2 tablespoons brown sugar
1 tablespoon, worcestershire sauce
Salt and pepper to taste

Cut steak in small pieces; dip in seasoned flour; brown on both sides. Place in bottom of casserole; top with sliced onion. Combine remaining ingredients and pour over steak. Cook at 350° for 2 hours.

Mattie Leyel, Clarkdale, Arizona

"Grandfather Munds was Jerome's first mayor. He and his family came West by wagon in 1876 and settled first in Prescott. In about a year they moved to the Verde Valley."

TINY SWEET-SOUR MEAT BALLS

1-1/2 pounds lean pork loin, ground
1 pound beef, ground
1 cup packaged dry bread crumbs
1/2 cup chopped almonds, browned, salted
2 eggs, beaten
3 tablespoons soy sauce

2 cloves garlic, crushed
Salt to taste
Dash of tabasco
Dash of nutmeg
Cornstarch for coating
Peanut oil, as needed

Thoroughly combine ingredients. Form into small balls the size of a quarter. Roll in cornstarch to coat. Fry slowly for 20 minutes. (See recipe for the sauce for these meat balls below.)

SAUCE FOR SWEET-SOUR MEAT BALLS

1 large can pineapple chunks, drained
1 cup pineapple juice
2 cups vinegar

1-1/2 cups sugar
1/2 cup soy sauce
4 tablespoons cornstarch

Mix pineapple juice, vinegar and soy sauce. Stir in sugar blended with cornstarch. Cook over low heat for 10 minutes, stirring constantly. Add meat balls. Serve in a chafing dish. Yields 30.

Mary Hufnagel, Tucson, Arizona

FRANKFURTER PIE

1 pound frankfurters, sliced 1/2-inch thick
1 onion, chopped
1/4 cup green pepper, chopped
1/2 cup celery, chopped
3 tablespoons butter, or margarine
1 teaspoon salt

1-1/2 cups mashed potatoes
2-1/2 tablespoons flour
1-1/4 cups milk
1 tablespoon worcestershire sauce
1/8 teaspoon pepper

Brown franks, onion, green pepper and celery in butter; blend in flour. Add milk and cook, stirring constantly until thickened. Add worcestershire sauce and seasonings. Pour into a greased 8-inch casserole and top with mashed potatoes. Bake in moderate 350° oven for 30 minutes. This frankfurter pie serves 6 people.

Deloros Santillan

SAUERKRAUT AND PORK CHOPS

Pork chops as needed
1 large can kraut
4 tablespoons shortening, or bacon grease
1/2 small onion, chopped
1 cup water

3 tablespoons green bell peppers, chopped
1 clove garlic, chopped
1/2 can tomato sauce
Salt and pepper to taste

Saute onions, green pepper and garlic in shortening until golden brown. Add tomato sauce and simmer for 5 minutes. Add kraut and water, salt and pepper, and cook over medium heat for 30 minutes. Then add 3 or 4 tablespoons of drippings from the browned pork chops. Combine all and simmer for 10 minutes and serve hot.

Sally Mongini

GERMAN SKILLET DINNER

1 tablespoon butter
1 can (14-ounce) sauerkraut
2/3 cup minute rice
1 medium onion, chopped

1 pound ground chuck
1-1/4 teaspoon salt
1/4 teaspoon pepper
2 cans (8-ounce) tomato sauce

Heat butter in large skillet. Spread sauerkraut over butter. Sprinkle with rice and onion. Top all with ground chuck, salt and pepper. Pour tomato sauce over top and cook covered over low heat 45 minutes.

Gen Schwalm

GERMAN BEEF BIRDS

1 beef round steak (about 2 pounds), cut 1/2-inch thick
6 smoked sausage links
2 tablespoons oil, or drippings
1 teaspoon salt

1 medium size onion, sliced
1 can (16-ounce) tomatoes
2 teaspoons caraway seeds
1 can (16-ounce) sauerkraut

Pound steak to 1/4-inch thickness. Cut into 6 serving pieces. Place a sausage link on each piece of steak and roll like a jelly roll. Fasten with wooden picks or skewers. Brown meat slowly in oil or drippings. Pour off drippings. Season with salt. Add onion, tomatoes, caraway seeds and liquid from sauerkraut, reserving sauerkraut to add later. Cover tightly and cook slowly for 1 hour. Add sauerkraut and continue to simmer 30 minutes longer, or until birds are tender. Yields 6 servings.

Beverly Sullivan

CHOCOLATE STEW

2 cups leftover meat, cubed
2 onions, sliced
1 egg
4 tablespoons flour
2 teaspoons prepared mustard
   (French's)

2 carrots, slivered
1 bay leaf
2 tablespoons sweet milk
2 tablespoons cocoa
Salt and pepper to taste
Wild rice or white rice

Saute the onions. Make batter of egg, flour, and enough water to make a thin batter. Dip the cubed leftover meat in the batter and brown. Add onions, carrots, salt and pepper, bay leaf, prepared mustard, and enough water to barely cover the mixture. Stew for 30 minutes by slow heat. Combine milk and cocoa and blend with 1/2 cup of the mixture before adding to the whole mixture. Return to same slow heat and cook for 10 minutes longer. Delicious served with wild rice or white rice.
                         Lydia Lloyd-Foster, Westport, Conn.

ENGLISH HOT POT

4 pork chops
2 potatoes, sliced
2 carrots, sliced
1 onion, sliced
1 cup water

Pour cup of water in baking pan. Place layer of sliced onions on bottom of pan, then a layer of potatoes, a layer of carrots; repeat until all the vegetables are used, seasoning each layer to taste. Place pork chops on top and sprinkle with salt and pepper. Bake 1 hour in 375° oven or until chops are done. If necessary, cover when chops have browned.
                                                Polly Warburton

PORK CHOP RICE CASSEROLE

5 to 6 pork chops
1 cup raw rice
2 cups beef bouillon
Garlic, salt, onion salt, pepper—to taste

Place chops in casserole. Sprinkle with seasoning salts and pepper. Sprinkle rice around, over and between chops. Pour bouillon over it all. Bake covered at 400° for 1 hour.
                                                          Fay Horton

HAMBURGER CHOP SUEY

2 medium size onions, chopped
1/4 cup shortening, salad oil
  or otherwise
1-1/2 pounds hamburger
1 bouillon cube
5 stalks celery, chopped
3/4 teaspoon salt
1 cup boiling water

3 tablespoons cornstarch
1/2 teaspoon brown sugar
1 tablespoon soy sauce
2 tablespoons water
1 can bean sprouts
1/4 teaspoon pepper
Chow mein noodles,
  or cooked rice

Peel onions and cut in thin slices. Cook in shortening along with the hamburger until meat is brown. Cut celery in thick slices and toss celery, bouillon cube dissolved in boiling water, salt and pepper into meat mixture. Cover and cook slowly for 10 minutes. Now make a smooth paste of cornstarch, brown sugar, soy sauce and water. Stir into meat and cook until sauce is slightly thick and clear. Add drained bean sprouts just long enough to heat through. Serve on chow mein noodles, or cooked rice.

Deloros Santillan

ROBERTA'S STEAK PIE

1 round steak, cubed
4 potatoes, diced
4 carrots, diced
1 onion, chopped
Garlic powder, salt, pepper, to taste
1 egg, beaten, to brush pie crust

1 teaspoon steak sauce
2 bouillon cubes
2 tablespoons flour
3/4 cup water
Shortening, as needed
Pie crust for topping

Flour the cubed steak and brown in a little shortening. Add potatoes, carrots, flour and bouillon cubes dissolved in the water. Also add salt, pepper, garlic powder and steak sauce. Simmer until thick. Pour into baking dish and top with pie crust. Brush pie crust with beaten egg. Sprinkle sesame seeds on the crust and bake in 350° oven until the steak pie is golden brown.   Roberta Westcott, Clarkdale, Arizona

THE LIFE SAVER — EMERGENCY MEAL FOR SIX

1 can (1-1/2 pounds) Libby's corn beef hash
9 eggs (Figuring on six persons—an egg and a half per person)
Onion, garlic powder, Lawry's seasoned salt, soy sauce—as desired
1/8 pound butter, or margarine

When you find yourself faced with six unexpected guests for supper -

Take the Libby's corn beef hash (other brands contain excess potatoes) and add the eggs. Thoroughly blend in a large bowl, using seasoning as you desire. After melting the fat in a large skillet, place the entire contents of the bowl in the skillet and stir constantly until good and hot. Along with the above serve a mixed green or vegetable salad, seasoned croutons, and toss well with a well seasoned Italian dressing; sour dough rolls or bread hot and buttered; and most important, this is to be served with a white wine well chilled.   John R. Walsh

NATIVE CHOW MEIN

2 pounds ground beef
1 can (16-ounce size) Chinese vegetables
1 onion, cut in 16 wedges
3 cups celery, sliced
1 can (4-ounce size) sliced mushrooms
1 can waterchestnuts, sliced
1 teaspoon salt
2 to 3 tablespoons cornstarch
2 tablespoons water
1/4 cup soy sauce
Chow Mein noodles
Rice as desired

Cook ground beef until lightly brown. Pour off dripping. Drain Chinese vegetables and mushrooms, reserving liquid to make 1-3/4 cups. Add the liquid to the ground beef. Add onions, celery and salt. Cover tightly and cook slowly for 15 minutes. Add Chinese vegetables, mushrooms and waterchestnuts. Mix cornstarch with water and soy sauce; add to the meat and vegetable mixture and continue cooking for 5 minutes, or until sauce is thick. Serve over rice. Top with chow mein noodles. Serve additional soy sauce with the chow mein. Makes 8 to 10 servings.

    Sandra Smull Holliday, Las Vegas, Nevada

TAGLIARINI - ITALIAN DINNER DISH

1 pound ground beef
3 teaspoons vegetable oil
1 teaspoon salt
3/4 cup onions, chopped
1 clove garlic, minced
3/4 cup green pepper, chopped
1 can (1-pound) tomatoes
1 can (10-ounce) whole kernel corn
  with its liquid
1 can (7-ounce) pitted ripe olives,
  drained and halved
1 package Italiano noodles
1-1/2 cups hot water

Brown meat in hot oil in large skillet. Stir in remaining ingredients, except cheese filling from noodles Italiano package. This dish can be prepared on top of range or in the oven. Cover and cook with low heat, stirring occasionally; takes about 25 minutes. Uncover and cook 10 to 15 minutes more. Stir in cheese filling during last minute. Makes 6 to 8 generous servings.

Mary Vojnic

SPAGHETTI SAUCE

1 pound ground beef
1 small onion, chopped fine
1 clove garlic
1 sliver bell pepper
1 piece celery, chopped
Pinch of oregano
Pinch of parsley
Rosemary to taste
1 can tomato paste
1 can (paste can) water
1 can (303 size) tomatoes
1 can mushrooms, bits
  and pieces
Salt and pepper
Pinch of cinnamon

In butter or margarine brown (do not burn) garlic and onion; add celery, bell pepper, parsley, oregano, and cook a few minutes. Add ground beef and brown; add paste and tomatoes; add water. Let cook very slowly at least 2-1/2 to 3 hours. Add mushrooms the last half hour of cooking period. Salt and pepper to taste and add cinnamon. Serve over hot spaghetti. Serves 6 to 8 persons.

Mickey Peterson

HAWAIIAN GOULASH

2 pounds ground chuck
2 medium size cans tomatoes
2 cans pineapple chunks
2 bell peppers, chopped
2 medium size onions,
  chopped
White rice, as needed
Salt and pepper

Saute onions and bell peppers. Add meat and brown. Add tomatoes and pineapple, also the juice from tomatoes and pineapple. Simmer about 25 minutes. Serve over white rice.

Mary Alice Alenius, Phoenix, Arizona

MINGUS MOUNTAIN CHICKEN

1/3 cup olive oil
3-pound chicken, cut in pieces
3/4 cup raw ham, diced
1 cup onions, sliced
2 cloves garlic, minced
3 medium tomatoes; peeled, chopped
2-1/2 cups water

2-1/2 cups raw rice
3/4 cup green pepper, chopped
1 small bay leaf
2-1/2 teaspoons salt
1/2 teaspoon cumin seed
1/8 teaspoon saffron
Pimento strips, as desired

Heat olive oil in a dutch oven; add chicken, ham, onions, garlic, and brown chicken on all sides. Add tomatoes; cover and simmer 20 minutes. Add remaining ingredients and bring to a boil. Lower the heat, cover and simmer slowly until rice is tender—about 20 minutes. Add more liquid, if necessary. Remove chicken, heap rice mixture in center of a large platter, and surround with the chicken. Garnish with strips of pimento as desired. Serves 6 to 8 and is an easy company dinner, as hostess may entertain guests while meal stays hot. Dish freezes well and is equally good as a leftover. For a perfect blend of flavors I serve with chilled red or white wine, grapefruit and avacado on fresh lettuce leaves topped with poppy seed dressing. With hot rolls and butter, a light dessert—such as a scoop of lime, orange and pineapple sherbet served with a small vanilla cookie—comprises a fine meal.

Connie Stevenson

HAMBURGER ONION PIE

1 cup and 2 tablespoons Bisquick
1/2 cup Carnation canned milk
1 pound ground beef
2 medium size onions
1 teaspoon salt

1/4 teaspoon pepper
1/2 teaspoon Accent
2 eggs
1 cup small curd cottage cheese

Mix together one cup Bisquick and canned milk. Knead gently 10 times. Roll dough to fit 9-inch pie pan. Saute beef and onions until meat has lost color; add salt, pepper, Accent and the 2 tablespoons of Bisquick. Spread in dough lined pie pan. Beat eggs slightly and blend in cottage cheese. Pour over meat mixture. Sprinkle with paprika. Bake 30 minutes in 375° oven. This can be made before and baked later. Makes 6 to 8 servings.

Ruth Hambley

"The Spanish Conquistadores first came here 35 years before the Pilgrims landed on the Plymouth Rock."

CHICKEN IN WINE SAUCE

2-1/2 pound fryer, cleaned, skinned, cut-up
2 tablespoons butter or margarine
1 large onion, minced
1/2 cup white wine
1 cup cold water
Salt and papper to taste

Heat butter in large skillet; add onion and fry until soft; add chicken pieces and brown lightly; add wine stirring gently until well mixed; add cold water and stir. Let this mixture simmer gently about 1 hour or until chicken is done. If too dry, add more water as needed to make a sauce. Serve with rice or mashed potatoes.   Ika Yurkovich

CREAMED TURKEY & HAM CASSEROLE

1/2 cup butter
1/2 cup flour
1 teaspoon salt
1/4 teaspoon pepper
2 cups milk

2 cups turkey or chicken broth
2 cups boiled ham cut Julienne style
4 cups cooked turkey, cubed
1/2 pound mushrooms, quartered
Cooked peas, as desired

Cook above ingredients for 10 minutes. In a large heavy saucepan melt all but 4 teaspoons of the butter; blend with flour, salt and pepper until smooth. Gradually stir in the milk and broth, stirring constantly until mixture is smooth and thickened. Add turkey and ham. In a heavy pan melt 4 teaspoons butter; add mushrooms and cook until tender. Place creamed mixture in a chafing dish, arrange mushrooms and peas around the edge. Delicious served in patty shells or on toast.
Dorothy King Goss

OVEN FRIED CHICKEN

1 fry chicken, cut up
Margarine, as needed
Potato chip crumbs, as needed
Salt and pepper to taste

Drop chicken pieces in melted margarine, then in potatochip crumbs. Arrange on cookie sheet, salt and pepper; bake in 375° oven for 1 hour or until done.   Marianne Wombacher, 9

BAKED CHICKEN BREASTS WITH WILD RICE

4 chicken breasts, halved and boned
1 cup regular long grain rice
2 or 3 tablespoons wild rice
1 small can sliced mushrooms, or
   a few ounces fresh mushrooms
Butter, or margarine, as needed

1 can cream of chicken soup
1 can cream of mushroom
1 can cream of celery soup
1 can of water

In shallow casserole about 10x15-inch place both white and wild rice. Combine soups and water in bowl and pour over rice. Dip chicken in melted butter, then roll in crushed corn flakes. Shape the coated chicken breasts into pillow-like forms and arrange them on top of the rice and soup mixture. Bake two hours at 300°; sprinkle with fresh chopped parsley and serve.
                    Katherine Michaelsen, daughter of Dr. & Mrs. J. R. Moore
                                                      Phoenix, AZ

VIVA LA CHICKEN

4 chicken breasts, cooked
12 corn tortillas
1 can cream of mushroom soup
1 can cream of chicken soup

2 cans green chili, salsa
1 cup milk
1 green onion, or 1/2 dry onion, minced
1 pound cheddar cheese

Prepare 24 hours in advance of serving. Bone chicken in large pieces. Cut tortillas in 1-inch strips. Mix soups, milk, salsa and onion. Grease large casserole and put chicken drippings on bottom of casserole. Then place 1/2 of the tortilla on bottom; add 1/2 of the chicken, then 1/2 of the sauce. Repeat. Refrigerate for 24 hours. Bake in 300° oven for 1-1/2 hours. Top with grated cheese before baking. Serves 6 to 8.
                                                                Marian Wombacher

OPULENT CHICKEN

4 chicken breasts
1 teaspoon paprika
1/2 pound fresh mushrooms, chopped
   or 4 ounces canned mushrooms
   or mixed fresh and canned mushrooms

2 tablespoons flour
1-1/2 teaspoons salt
1/4 cup Sherry wine
1/2 cup margarine
2/3 cup chicken consomme

Sprinkle chicken with salt and paprika. Brown in 4 tablespoons margarine and arrange in casserole. Put another 4 tablespoons margarine in same skillet and saute mushrooms for 5 minutes. Sprinkle the flour over them and stir in the consomme and wine. Simmer for 5 more minutes. Pour this sauce over the chicken. Cover and bake at 375° for 45 minutes.
                                                                 Hazel Statzell

VEGETABLE DISHES

ZUCCHINI CASSEROLE

1-1/2 pounds zucchini squash
2 tablespoons butter, or margarine
1 cup onions, minced
1 clove garlic, minced
1 cup instant rice
1 pound ground beef
2/3 cup water

1-1/2 teaspoons basil
1 pint creamed cottage cheese
1 can (10-1/2-ounce) tomato soup
1 cup sharp American cheese, shredded

Cut zucchini into 1/4-inch slices and cook in small amount of boiling water until barely tender. Drain well. Melt butter in skillet; add the onion and garlic; stir until onion is tender but not browned. Add meat and cook until meat begins to brown. Stir in rice and basil. Spread half of the zucchini slices in a greased 2-1/2-quart casserole. Top with meat mixture, then cottage cheese and the remaining zucchini. Combine soup and water and pour over casserole contents. Sprinkle with cheese and bake at 350° for 35 to 45 minutes, or until heated through and lightly browned on top. Makes 6 to 8 servings. Serve with tossed salad and French bread. Your guests will want your recipe.

Ruth Sullivan

"The area's mining history extends back to 1125 A. D., when Indians mined salt in the nearby Verde Valley."

EGGPLANT CASSEROLE

1 large eggplant, sliced in rounds
1 egg, beaten
Flour, as needed
1-1/2 cups white sauce, or 1 can cream soup
1 cup white cheese, grated
1 pound ground round
1 small onion, chopped
1 cup canned tomatoes
1 teaspoon oregano
Salt, pepper, cooking oil

Dip eggplant in egg and flour seasoned with salt and pepper. Brown in oil and drain. Make a white sauce from basic recipe, or use 1 can of cream soup. Brown the meat and onions in oil. Add tomatoes, salt, pepper, oregano; and let simmer 10 to 15 minutes. In a casserole dish layer the eggplant, meat, white sauce and cheese. Repeat until all ingredients are used. Add strips of ortega green chili for extra zip. Place in oven and bake at 350° for 30 to 45 minutes. Serves 6 people.

Ava Gutierrez

EGGPLANT PARMIGIANA

2 tablespoons oil
1 small onion, chopped
1 clove garlic, crushed
1 green pepper, cut in strips
1 pound ground beef
3 cups canned tomatoes
1 tablespoon parsley, chopped
1/4 teaspoon oregano
Salt and pepper to taste
1 medium eggplant
1 cup bread crumbs
1/2 cup grated Parmesan cheese
1/2 pound Mozzarella or Cheddar cheese, sliced

Heat oil and add onion, garlic, green pepper and beef. Stir occasionally until onion is tender but not brown and meat has lost its red color. Add tomatoes, parsley, oregano and salt and pepper to taste. Simmer uncovered 30 minutes or until slightly thickened. Peel eggplant and cut into 1/2-inch slices. Cook in 1/2 cup oil until soft and lightly browned on both sides. Season with salt and pepper. Mix bread crumbs, cheese, salt and pepper to taste. Alternate layers of eggplant, bread crumbs and cheese mixture and tomato and beef mixture in 1-1/2 quart baking dish, beginning and ending with eggplant. Top with cheese and tomato mixture. Bake 375° for 20 minutes.

Sally Grigg Crawford, Bishop, California

"Jerome was incorporated in 1899 as the fifth largest city in Arizona."

SQUASH AND POTATO CASSEROLE

Zucchini squash, sliced thin
Cream of celery soup
Potatoes, sliced thin
Parsley leaves, chopped
Margarine as needed
Parmesan cheese as desired

Place zucchini squash in a casserole dish; spread with a small amount of the soup; make layers until all is used up; top with the parsley, a bit of margarine and grated Parmesan cheese, as desired. Cover and bake at 350° until tender, which takes about 1 hour.

Nina Antonelli

NEW ENGLAND SUCCOTASH

1 large can (1 pound 11 ounce) baked beans (I use B&M brand)
1 large can (1 pound 12 ounce) Niblets or Mexicorn
1/4 pound bacon, cut in strips
1 large onion, sliced
1 tablespoon brown sugar

Layer into beanpot or casserole. Bake 1 hour or longer at 350°. This is great for picnics. Only one complaint from hungry grandchildren— "There isn't any more!"

Winifred S. Foster

SCALLOPED CORN AND CLAMS

1 can of minced clams
1 can (No.2 size) cream style corn
1/2 tablespoon onions, chopped
2 slices of crisp fried bacon, crumbled
2 tablespoons bacon fat
2 beaten eggs
1/2 cup evaporated milk, undiluted
1 cup cracker crumbs, rolled
Salt and pepper to taste

Save 1/4 cup of cracker crumbs for the top, but mix the rest with the other ingredients and pour them into a greased casserole. Bake in oven at 350° for about 35 minutes, or until set in center.

Inez Kelly

SKILLET SQUASH SCRAMBLE

6 to 8 small zucchini squash
1 medium onion, chopped
2 tablespoons butter
3 ripe tomatoes, peeled and cut in wedges
4 to 6 eggs, beaten
1 cup cheddar cheese, diced
Salt and pepper

Heat butter in large skillet. Clean and slice squash. Brown squash and onion slowly for 5 to 10 minutes. Add tomatoes, cover, and cook about 5 minutes. Add beaten eggs, cheese, salt and pepper to taste. Cover and cook over low heat until cheese melts and eggs are firm. Serve this squash scramble immediately.

Nina Antonelli
Detroit, Michigan

SWEETPOTATO BALLS

8 medium size sweet potatoes (not yams)
12 large marshmallows
Corn flakes, as needed
Spry, as needed

Peel, cook and mash potatoes. Make a ball around a marshmallow—about 2 inches in diameter. Roll in crushed corn flakes. Brown in a skillet in 1/2-inch deep hot Spry. Makes approximately 12 balls.

Virginia Mick

BATTER COATED FRUIT OR VEGETABLES

1 cup flour (sifted)
1 teaspoon baking powder
1/2 teaspoon salt
1 egg slightly beaten
1 cup milk

Bananas cut in 1-inch chunks
Cauliflower separated into flowerettes
Eggplant cut into strips
Onion rings
1 quart corn oil

Sift dry ingredients together. Mix egg, 1/4 cup of the corn oil and milk and add to dry ingredients. Dry the vegetables or fruit and dust with flour. Dip into batter. Drain on rack or waxed paper. Heat rest of oil to 375° and fry the prepared fruit or vegetables until brown. Drain on absorbent paper.

Fay Horton

STUFFED CABBAGE IN TOMATO SAUCE

1 pound lean ground beef
1 cup rice, cooked
1 small onion, chopped
1 egg
1/2 teaspoon caraway seed
1/2 teaspoon salt
1/4 teaspoon pepper
1 head cabbage
1 can (8-ounce) tomato sauce
1 cup water
Wesson oil, as needed

First steam the whole head of cabbage; cut out the center; trim off the thickest part of stem from cabbage leaves to make it easier to roll. Mix meat mixture thoroughly. Divide into small portions and wrap each into a leaf. Brown cabbage rolls in Wesson oil. Add contents of can of tomato sauce; and 1 cup water. Cover and cook slowly 40 minutes.
       Olga Svob Dugan, Downey, California

BRUSSEL SPROUTS

2 packages frozen brussel sprouts
1 tablespoon butter
1/4 teaspoon ginger
1 can (15-ounce) white seedless grapes, or
 1 package frozen brussel sprouts, and
 1 can (8-ounce) white seedless grapes

Cook brussel sprouts with salt, butter and ginger until done. Add the drained white seedless grapes. Bring to a boil again and serve hot.
       Ruth Hambley

GREEN BEAN CASSEROLE

1 can (16-ounce) French style green string beans (reserve 1/4 cup juice)
1/2 can French fried onions
1 can mushroom soup, diluted with the 1/4 cup bean juice
1/2 cup shrp cheddar cheese, grated
1 can water chestnuts, chopped coarsely
1/2 cup of sliced almonds

Mix all ingredients together thoroughly and pour into a buttered casserole, top with crumbled French fried onions and almonds, and bake at 350° for 30 to 50 minutes.   Anna Lou Antrim

MASHED POTATO MIRACLE

3 cups water
1 teaspoon salt
5 tablespoons butter
1 medium size onion, minced
1 package (6-ounce) cream cheese
1 can, as desired, French fried onions
2-3/4 cups potato flakes
1/2 cup milk

Bring water to boil. Add butter and stir in potato flakes. Add onion and cream cheese. Add milk until potatoes are soft and fluffy. Put in large casserole and top with French-fried onions. Bake in a very slow (125°) oven, or as low as possible, for 45 minutes. Delicious golden crust and creamy flavor are the miracle factors!   Frankie Vincent

GERMAN RED CABBAGE

1 medium head of red cabbage, shredded
8 slices of bacon, diced
1 medium onion, diced
2 cloves
8 to 10 whole peppers, ground (optional)
2 cups red dry wine

In a 2-quart saucepan try the bacon; add the onion and cook until the onion is glazed. Add cabbage and cook until cabbage is wilted; then add peppers, cloves and wine. Put lid on pan and simmer for 2 to 3 hours. Serve with goose or duck.   Liz Pecharich

SPEEDY BAKED BEANS

4 strips bacon, diced
1 large onion, minced
2 cans (No. 1 tall) Campbell's pork and beans
1 teaspoon mustard, prepared
1/4 cup chili
1 small can pineapple chunks, if desired

Saute bacon until crisp; add onion and cook until onion is yellow. Stir in the pork and beans, mustard and chili sauce. Pour into greased 1-1/2 quart casserole. Bake uncovered in moderate 350° oven for 45 minutes or until beans are brown and bubbly. Serve hot. For variation, add a small can of pineapple chunks. (Sent by a Jerome native):
Olga Svob Dugan, Downey, California

EGGPLANT ITALIENNE

1 eggplant
1/2 pound or more of mozerella cheese
1 pound ground meat
Salt and pepper to taste

Slice and peel the eggplant. It can be dipped in seasoned flour and fried first, if you prefer. Ground meat should be sauted lightly, but kept moist. Thinly slice the mozerella cheese. The meat should be salted and peppered to taste while sauteing. Lightly grease a casserole and put in a layer of eggplant, a layer of meat, then a layer of cheese. Last, a layer of spaghetti sauce (see recipe below). Add layers until all ingredients are used or until casserole is filled. I reverse the last two layers, as I prefer the cheese on top. Bake in a moderate oven 30 to 40 minutes, or till nice and bubbly.

SPAGHETTI SAUCE

1/2 teaspoon black pepper
1/4 cup olive oil
1 onion, minced
3 tablespoons tomato paste
1/2 cup water
3 cups drained tomatoes
1 bay leaf
1/2 cup cheese, grated
1 tablespoon sugar

Add the pepper to the oil and cook the onion in this till brown. Mix the tomato paste with the water and add in three installments to the oil and the onion, cooking till all are blended. Add the drained tomatoes, bay leaf and salt. Cook 30 minutes, then add sugar and cook for 15 minutes longer.
                                                                                                      Ruth Corlett

"Jerome was burned out three times between 1897 and 1899. One fire inspired jeering headlines in a Prescott paper. JEROME BURNS AGAIN! ENTIRE BUSINESS DISTRICT OF 24 SALOONS AND 14 CHINK RESTAURANTS DESTROYED!"

LIMA BEANS AND ZUCCHINI CASSEROLE

1 package (10-ounce) frozen small lima beans
Boiling salt water
4 medium zucchinis
1 can (4-ounce) sliced mushrooms, drained
1 can mushroom soup
1/4 cup onions, minced
1/4 teaspoon salt
2 teaspoons parsley, chopped
1/3 cup sliced almonds — (optional)
1 tablespoon butter, melted

Cook lima beans in salt water for 5 minutes. Drain. Turn into greased casserole—the 1-1/2 quart size. Slice zucchini in thin slices and add to casserole with mushrooms and mushroom soup, onions, salt and parsley. Mix until blended. Cover and bake 35 minutes at 350°; then remove from oven and add chopped almonds that have been mixed with butter. The zucchini seems to stay crisp. Serves 6 to 8 people.

Phyllis Miller

BARBECUED LIMAS

2 pounds lima beans, soaked overnight
1/4 pound salt pork
3 onions
1 clove garlic
4 tablespoons fat
2 cans tomato soup
1 cup liquor from beans
A little sugar
2 tablespoons prepared mustard
1/4 cup chili sauce
2 tablespoons Worcestershire sauce
1-1/2 teaspoons chili powder
1 teaspoon salt
1/3 cup vinegar

Cook limas with salt pork until done. Saute onions and garlic in fat. Add tomato soup and liquor from beans. Blend mustard, chili sauce, Worcestershire sauce, chili powder, salt, vinegar and sugar. Add to tomato mixture and simmer 30 minutes. Add to drained beans and bake at 350° for 1 hour.

Ellen Vojnic

SPINACH AND RICE CASSEROLE

2 packages frozen chopped spinach
1 cup rice, brown or minute
1 can mushroom soup
2 eggs, well beaten
1-1/2 cups milk
Salt, pepper and paprika to taste
Butter, cheese, as needed

Beat eggs until light; add mushroom soup, cooked spinach, rice and milk. Pour into buttered casserole; sprinkle with grated cheese, butter and paprika. Bake at 350° for 30 minutes, or until firm.

Muriel O'Boyle, Santa Rosa, California

BREADED CAULIFLOWER

1 large cauliflower
2 or 3 eggs, depending on size
Soda cracker crumbs, crushed
Crisco and cooking oil, as needed
Salt and pepper to taste

Separate cauliflower flowerettes; if too large, cut in half. Wash thoroughly and boil in salted water until tender; about 15 minutes. Do not overcook. Drain and let cool. Salt and pepper the eggs and beat with fork. Dip the flowerettes into eggs and then roll in crumbs. Fry in pan with Crisco and cooking oil. Have shortening at least 1 inch deep. Fry until a golden brown on all sides.   Mickey Peterson

BAKED ZUCCHINI CASSEROLE

1 pound Zucchini squash
1 medium size onion
2 tablespoons butter
1 cup half-and-half cream

2 eggs, beaten
1/2 cup sharp cheese, grated
1 can cream style corn
Salt and pepper to taste

Boil the zucchini squash until barely tender; drain well. Saute onion in butter. Mix all ingredients except the zucchini. Put half of the cooked zucchini in casserole dish; add half of the mixture; repeat. Bake at 300° for 1 hour. Serves 5 or 6 people.   Zella Davis

POTATOES AU GRATIN

4 or 5 potatoes, boiled in jackets
White sauce
Salt and pepper
2 cups or more Cheddar cheese

Make the white sauce and season to taste. Grate the cheese; peel the boiled potatoes and slice. In a shallow pan put a layer of potatoes, a layer of white sauce and a layer of cheese, repeating the layers until all the ingredients are added. Bake at 350° till cheese is melted and brown on top.   Ruth Cantrell

PLANTATION POTATOES

2 pounds frozen southern style hash brown potatoes, partially thawed
1/4 cup coarsely chopped green pepper
1 jar (2-ounce) pimientos, sliced, drained and chopped
2 cups milk
1-1/4 teaspoons salt

3/4 cup fine dry bread crumbs
1/3 cup soft butter
2/3 cup (3 ounces) sharp process American cheese, shredded

Put potatoes in a buttered 2-quart baking dish, separating potato pieces. Add green pepper and pimiento; mix lightly. Combine milk and salt; pour over potatoes. Cover with foil. Bake in moderate oven 350° for 1-1/4 hours, or until potatoes are fork tender. Remove foil; top with mixture of bread crumbs, butter and cheese. Continue baking for 15 minutes, or until cheese is melted. Makes 6 servings.

Beverly Sullivan

POTATOES MARGARET

1 cup dairy sour cream
1/2 cup milk
1 tablespoon onion, minced
5 cups cooked potatoes, sliced

Salt and pepper
1 tablespoon butter
2 tablespoons fine dry bread crumbs

Combine cream, milk and onion; place half of potatoes in greased baking dish; sprinkle generously with salt and pepper; add half of the sour cream mixture; repeat layers. Melt butter, add crumbs and toss to mix. Sprinkle over top of baking dish mixture; bake in moderate 350° oven for 20 to 25 minutes. Makes 6 servings.

John Croun

MEXICAN DISHES

CHILIES RELLENOS WITH SAUCE

1 can (4-ounce) chili oretega (4 chilies)
1/2 pound longhorn cheese, grated
3 eggs, separated
1/2 cup all-purpose flour
Oil for deep fryer
Salt and pepper to taste

Remove seed from chili, if any. Stuff chilies with grated cheese. Beat egg whites in a medium size bowl until stiff. Fold in slightly beaten egg yolks with 2 tablespoons flour into the beaten egg whites and continue to fold in until no patches of white remain. Add salt and pepper to remaining flour. Roll cheese-stuffed chili in flour and dip in egg batter; place in deep fat fryer with oil heated to $400°$ and fry until golden brown on all sides. Serve hot. (See sauce recipe below)

Geraldine Gutierrez

SAUCE FOR CHILIES RELLENOS

1 cup canned stewed tomatoes
1 small onion, diced
1/4 teaspoon oregano, ground
Salt and pepper to taste

Combine all ingredients in one saucepan and simmer 10 to 15 minutes, stirring occasionally. Pour over chilies rellenos. Geraldine Gutierrez

TAMALE PIE

1 cup cornmeal
1-1/2 cups milk
1 tablespoon chili powder
Ripe olives, as desired
1/4 cup salad oil
1 large onion, diced

1 clove garlic, diced
1-1/2 pounds hamburger, a good grade
1 pint tomato puree
1 can (16-ounce) creamed corn
1 tablespoon salt

Mix cornmeal, milk and chili powder and let stand. Fry onions and garlic in salad oil. Add meat and brown. Then add tomato puree and corn and cook thoroughly. Add cornmeal mixture and salt. Add ripe olives, if desired. Pour into greased baking dish; a long, flat pan is best. Bake 45 minutes in moderate oven. Sprinkle with cheese and cook 10 minutes longer. This is Yi Brown's recipe and is submitted in her memory.
Irene McDonald, Flagstaff, Arizona

CHILI VERDE Y QUESO

2 cans (4-ounce size) ortega green chilies, drained
1 pound monterey jack cheese, coarsely grated
2/3 cup canned milk, undiluted
1 tablespoon flour
1 pound cheddar cheese, coarsely grated
2 medium tomatoes or canned tomatoes, sliced

4 egg whites
4 egg yolks
1/2 teaspoon salt
1/8 teaspoon pepper

Pre-heat oven to 325°. Remove seeds from chilies and dice them. In a large bowl combine the grated cheese and green chilies. Turn into a well buttered shallow 2-quart casserole 2x8x12. In large bowl with electric mixer at high speed, beat egg whites just until stiff peaks form, when beater is slowly raised. In small bowl combine egg yolks, milk, flour, salt and pepper; and mix until well blended. Using rubber scraper, gently fold beaten whites into egg yolk mixture in casserole; and using a fork, ooze it through the cheese. Bake 30 minutes. Remove from oven and arrange sliced tomatoes over-lapping around edge of casserole. Bake 30 minutes longer, or until a silver knife inserted comes out clean. If desired, garnish with a sprinkling of chopped green chilies. Makes 8 to 10 servings. When served with a tossed green salad or coleslaw and crisp tortillas, it makes a complete meal.
Dorothy Smith

CALABACITAS ESPECIAL (SPECIAL ZUCCHINI)

1 small onion, chopped
4 to 6 medium size zucchini, cubed
2 tablespoons cooking oil
2 fresh tomatoes, chopped; or 1 cup canned tomatoes
1 can whole kernel corn
1 cup yellow longhorn cheese, grated
1 cup water or broth

Saute onion and zucchini in oil; add tomatoes, corn and liquid. Season to taste. Steam until squash is tender. Drain; add cheese and serve. Serves 6 people.

Ava Gutierrez

CHILI CON CARNE

1 pound ground beef
1 large onion, chopped fine
2 cloves garlic, minced
2 tablespoons hot shortening
2 tablespoons chili powder
1 teaspoon cumin powder

1 teaspoon salt
1/4 teaspoon pepper
2 cans tomato sauce
1 can water
4 cups cooked pinto beans

Cover pinto beans with water and simmer for one hour. (2 cups of dry pinto beans cook up into 4 cups, as required for this recipe.) Brown beef, onion and garlic in hot fat; add chili powder, cumin, salt, pepper, tomato sauce and water; simmer all with meat mixture 20 to 25 minutes; then add the cooked pinto beans and finish cooking.

Joan Radetich Cirata, Palm Springs, California

CHILI BEANS

1 pound pinto beans
1 pound ground beef
1 tablespoon garlic powder
1 tablespoon cumin seed
1 tablespoon cumin powder

2 tablespoons chili pepper
1 tablespoon paprika
1 tablespoon salt

Cook beans covered with water until tender. Brown ground beef; when browned, mix all other ingredients until well blended. Add to beans and simmer about 1 hour.

Margaret Cambruzzi

MEXICAN CORN BREAD (SAME RECIPE IN SPANISH BELOW)

2 cans cream corn	4 eggs
1/3 cup oil	1/2 teaspoon baking soda
2 cups yellow corn meal	2 teaspoons salt
3/4 cup milk	2 cans green chili
	2 cups longhorn cheese, grated

First mix in a large bowl the corn meal, baking powder, salt. Add milk, whole eggs beaten with a fork, oil and creamed corn. Take a large bread or cake pan and rub with oil. Put half of the mixture in oiled pan, then top with strips of green chili and half of the cheese. Add the other half of mixture and put in remainder of green chili, covering well with the rest of the cheese. Bake in oven 375° for 1 hour (in Jerome's mile-high altitude) or 45 minutes at lower altitudes.

Cleofas Ortiz

PAN de MAIZ MEXICANO

2 latas maiz de crema	4 huevos
1/3 tasa de ascete	1/2 cucharita de sosa
2 tasas de harina de maiz	2 cucharitas de sal
3/4 tasas de leche	2 latas de chili verde
	2 tasas de queso rajado amarillo

Primero revuelvase en tasa grande, la harina de Maiz, sosa, y sal. Añadirse la leche, huevos enteros batidos con un tenedor, aceite y Maiz de crema. Tome una bandeja de pan o pastel y se unta con aceite. Ponga la mitad de este material revuelto, en la bendeja enaceitada, y luego ponga tiras chiquas de chile verde y la mitad del queso sobre el material en la bandeja. Ponga la otra mitad del material arriba de eso y lo que queda del chile verde, cubriendo todo con el restante del queso. Se cocina en el horno de 375 grados por una hora en Jerome; 45 minutos en otras alturas bajas.

Cleofas Ortiz

HUEVOS RANCHEROS — ONE SERVING

1/3 cup cooked green chili sauce
2 eggs, fried or poached
1 tortilla, snack size
Monterey Jack cheese, grated

Soften tortilla on hot, slightly greased, griddle; it should not be crisp. Place eggs on tortilla, top with green chili sauce and sprinkle with cheese. This is a real wake-me-up breakfast.

Karen Brown

EMPANADAS (Meat Turnovers)

1 tablespoon butter
1 tablespoon sugar
3 teaspoons baking powder
1/2 teaspoon salt

1 cup flour
3/4 cup milk
2 eggs, well beaten

Cream butter and sugar and add beaten eggs. Sift together flour, baking powder and salt. Add dry ingredients alternately with the milk to the egg batter. Mix to a stiff dough. Toss on a floured board and roll very thin. Cut in sizes of pancakes and spread with the meat mixture given below. Roll over like jelly roll and fry to a golden brown in very deep fat. Serve with a green chili sauce.

MEAT MIXTURE FOR EMPANADAS

1-1/4 pounds ground pork
1/2 green pepper, diced
1/2 cup onion, minced
1/4 teaspoon thyme
Salt to taste
2 cups water
1 cup pineapple, diced

Mix well and fry to a deep brown. Spread on each piece of the dough; roll up and fry. Or roll the dough out as for pie crust; spread evenly with meat mixture; roll over as for a jelly roll; and bake brown in a slow oven with diced pineapple and the water poured over it.

Isabel Magill

GREEN CHILI SAUCE (Salso de Chili Verde)
(Use over empanadas, if desired)

5 large green bell peppers
2 green tomatoes
2 large onions
2 buttons of garlic
1/2 cup vinegar
1/2 cup olive oil (or 2 tablespoons lard

1 large cucumber, unpeeled
1 cup water
2 tablespoons sugar
1/2 teaspoon ground cinnamon
1/2 teaspoon ground cloves
1 teaspoon salt

Run vegetables through a fine grinder. Have oil or lard heating. Put the vegetables, spices, vinegar, sugar, salt and water into it. Cook 15 minutes and serve over empanadas or other meat or eggs.

Isabel Magill

ACAPULCO CORN BREAD

1 cup buttermilk
1/2 teaspoon soda
1 teaspoon salt
3 teaspoons baking powder
2 eggs, beaten
1 can cream corn
1 cup cornmeal

1/4 cup salad oil
1 small onion, minced
1 can (4-ounce) ortega chilies
1-1/2 cup longhorn cheese, or a sharp cheddar cheese

Combine buttermilk, soda, baking powder and salt. Add eggs, corn, cornmeal, oil and onion. Spread half of the batter in a well greased 8 x 12-inch baking dish or skillet. Open the chilies flat and remove the seeds. Cover the half of batter in the skillet with the chilies and 3/4 cup of the cheese. Top with the remaining batter and cover with the remaining cheese. Bake at 350° for 1 hour. Serves 8 people.

Dorothy Smith, Redding, California

MEXICAN CORN BREAD

2 eggs
3/4 cup milk
1/3 cup oil
1 can (8-ounce) cream style corn
1 cup yellow cornmeal
1 teaspoon baking powder
1/2 teaspoon salt
1/2 teaspoon soda

3 ortega green chilies, chopped, or 1/2 can chopped chilies
3/4 cup cheddar cheese, grated, or more, if desired

This is good to serve with soup. Beat egg; add milk, corn and oil. Sift dry ingredients and combine. Pour 1/2 of the batter into greased pan size 1-1/2 x 8 x 11 inches. Sprinkle with chilies and cheese. Pour rest of batter on top and sprinkle with cheese. Bake at 400° for 30 minutes.

Olga Berg Clarkdale, AZ

"The first automobile to come to Jerome was bought jointly by Dr. Hawkins and Walter Miller in 1903, and shipped by rail to Prescott. Old timers say it was a Franklin. Mr. Miller took delivery, driving it to Jerome via Dewey and the Cherry Creek road. The trip was made without serious trouble--at a speed of 11 miles per hour, a record of which Walter was quite proud."

ALBONDIGAS (MEAT BALLS, MEXICAN STYLE)

1-1/2 pounds round ground meat
1 small bunch green onions
Cilantro (Coreander seed) enough to spice it
Rice—small amount—about 1/2 cup
1 large tomato, peeled and cut up in pieces

Add salt and pepper to ground meat, handful of dry rice. Make into small balls. Saute chopped green onion, coreander and tomato in a little lard. Add hot water to make broth. Drop in meat balls and cook about 45 minutes. Bouillon square or 1 can consomme can be used, enough water to make it soupy.

Chonita Lawrence

BILLY HUNZICKER'S TAMALA LOAF

1 pound hamburger
1 onion, chopped
1 pepper, chopped
1 tablespoon Crisco

1 tablespoon chili powder
1 cup tomato sauce
1 teaspoon salt
1 quart corn meal, cooked

Cook meat, onion and pepper in Crisco. Add chili powder, tomato sauce and salt. Line a casserole dish with 1 quart cooked corn meal mush (very stiff). Fill with the meat mixture. Bake at 375° for 20 to 30 minutes. (This recipe was found in Dorothy Larson's cookbook.)

"Fritz" Larson, Owego, New York

CHICKEN TORTILLA BAKE

6 to 8 flour or corn tortillas (6" size)
1-1/2 to 2 cups cubed chicken or turkey
1 can condensed cream of chicken soup
1 can (4-ounce) green chilies
1 cup grated Monterey Jack cheese
Salt and pepper to taste
SlicedSpanish olives as desired

Heat tortillas in a greased skillet just enough to soften and layer a flat dish or a 1-3/4 quart casserole dish. Layer with chicken, soup, chilies and cheese; then repeat until ingredients are used. Top with sliced Spanish olives. Bake 1/2 hour at 325° and serve with hot sauce, if desired. Serves 2 to 4.

Karen Brown

SPANISH MACARONI

2 stalks celery
1 long green chili
1 medium sized onion
1 tablespoon parsley, chopped
Corn oil, as needed
1 can (14-1/2-ounce) tomatoes (pear-shaped Contadina)
1 can (8-ounce) tomato sauce
1 sauce can water
1/2 teaspoon rosemary leaves, crushed
1/4 teaspoon thyme powder
1/2 teaspoon savory
1/8 teaspoon oregano
1/8 teaspoon marjoram
1 teaspoon chili powder
4 cups (left over roast) meat, chopped
1-1/2 cups Mostaccioli macaroni
10 ounces cracker barrel sharp cheese, grated with coarse grater
8 saltine crackers, rolled

Chop celery, green chili, onion and parsley with a knife or the coarse blade of your grinder. Saute in a small amount of corn oil till wilted but not browned. Add tomatoes, water, meat and seasonings; simmer 30 minutes, adding more water if it gets too dry. Cook the macaroni till soft. Grease bottom and sides of oblong baking dish. Put a layer of macaroni in bottom, then a layer of cheese over it. Now put the meat in and press it down. Add rest of macaroni on top of meat, then plenty of cheese. Cover with the cracker crumbs. Pour fresh milk over the top and cut down through with a case knife so the milk will go through and moisten the loaf. Cook slowly; about 1-1/2 hours in 350° oven.

Myrtle Boyd

TORTILLAS

3 cups flour
1/2 teaspoon salt
1/2 cup lard
1 tablespoon baking powder
1 to 1-1/2 cups hot water, as needed

Mix all dry ingredients together, add water a little at a time and knead until it forms a medium soft ball. Form individual balls. Roll out round with rolling pin until desired circle size. Cook on top of grill on both sides.

Al Robles, Jr., 7

TIA JUANA TAMALE

1/2 cup oil
1 onion, chopped
1 clove garlic, minced
1 pound hamburger
2 teaspoons chili powder
2-1/2 teaspoons salt
1 can (No. 2-1/2) whole tomatoes
1 cup cornmeal
1 cup milk
1 can (No. 2) cream corn
1 cup ripe olives, chopped

Saute onions and garlic in oil for 5 minutes; then add beef and brown. Add salt, chili and tomatoes; cover and cook for 15 minutes. Stir in cornmeal and milk and cook another 15 minutes, stirring frequently. Add corn and olives. Pack into 2 greased loaf pans; brush top with oil and bake 1 hour at 325°. Top with shredded longhorn cheese about the last 5 minutes of baking.   Marian Wombacher

TACO BEAN CASSEROLE

16-ounce can of pork and beans
1 pound cooked hamburger
7-1/2-ounce can taco sauce
2 tablespoons onions, chopped
1 can beef broth
1 cup ripe olives, diced
1/2 pound cheese, shredded
5-1/2-ounce package taco chips, crumbled

Mix beans, meat, broth, taco sauce and onions. Let stand for 10 minutes. Put taco chips, cheese and olives over mixture. Bake 30 minutes at 350°.
                                                                Ruth Wilkinson

MEXICAN CORN BREAD

1 cup yellow cornmeal
1 can (8-3/4-ounce) cream style corn
3/4 cup milk
1/2 teaspoon soda
1/4 cup shortening, liquid
2 eggs
1 small can ortego chili, diced
2 cups cheddar cheese, grated

Stir all ingredients together, but save part of the cheese to spread on top. Bake in 9x13-inch pan in 400° oven for 45 minutes. Myrtle Boyd

TAMALE LOAF

1 pound fresh pork, cut up
1 large can tomato puree
1 can corn
1 small can ripe olives, cut up
1 cup Wesson oil
1 large onion, cut up
2 teaspoons salt
3 tablespoons chili powder
2 cups yellow corn meal
2 eggs, beaten
1 cup milk

Cook the pork in the oil, adding onion and salt; then the corn, tomato puree, olives and chili powder. In a separate container mix corn meal, eggs and milk; add to first mixture and mix all together. Bake for 1 hour in a moderate oven. Serves 12 people.

Grace Moore

GREEN CHILI ENCHILADAS

2 cups turkey, chopped
1 can (4-ounce) green chili, diced
1 pound longhorn cheese, grated
1 onion, chopped
1 can (4-ounce) ripe olives, chopped
2 dozen corn tortillas
1 pound can enchilada sauce
1/2 cup cheese, grated

Mix first 5 ingredients. Soften tortillas one at a time in hot oil; dip each in enchilada sauce; roll small amount of turkey mixture into each tortilla and place in baking dish. Do not stack enchiladas. Sprinkle remaining cheese on top of enchiladas. Put in a 350° oven until cheese is melted; takes 10 or 15 minutes.

Sally Grigg Crawford

FLAUTITAS WITH FILLING

6 or 12 corn or flour tortillas
3 pounds flank or chuck roast
1/2 pound mild cheddar cheese
1 onion, chopped
2 cloves garlic, chopped fine
2 avacados
1 teaspoon salt
1 teaspoon pepper
1/2 cup canned tomatoes
1/2 teaspoon oregano
1/2 teaspoon cumin
1/2 teaspoon chili, green or red

Boil meat until tender; cool and chop; mix with other ingredients (except avacados and lettuce) and then fry. Spread tortillas with this mixture and fry in deep fat. Garnish with lettuce and avacado.

Pat Tisnado Robles

CAKES & COOKIES

WELSH CAKES

3 cups sifted flour
1 cup sugar
1-1/2 teaspoons baking powder
1-1/4 teaspoons soda
2 teaspoons nutmeg

1 cup shortening
1 cup currants
2 eggs
6 tablespoons milk

Sift dry ingredients into medium size bowl. Cut in shortening with pastry blender or two knives until crumbly; add currants. Beat eggs and milk in bowl just until blended; add to fruit and flour mixture. Mix well (dough will be stiff). Cover and chill one to two hours. Divide dough in thirds and roll out each third 1/4 inch thick on a lightly floured board. Cut into rounds with a large cookie cutter. Heat griddle very slowly. Test temperature by sprinkling a few drops of water on the griddle. When drops bounce around, the temperature is right. Grease lightly before each baking. Bake cookies slowly, a few at a time, until tops puff and turn shiny; turn and bake other side until golden. Cool on wire rack; when cold, store in tightly covered container. These cakes are fruity, moist and real old-fashioned. Perfect for school lunch, tea, or with fruit dessert. Recipe yields 3 dozen.

Ruth Sullivan

"In 1894 construction was started on the narrow gauge railway from Chino Valley to Jerome."

CHOCOLATE CAKE

1 stick butter, or margarine
2 cups sugar
3/4 cup cocoa
Pinch of salt
Boiling water, as needed

2 cups flour
1 cup buttermilk
1 teaspoon soda
3 eggs, separated
1 teaspoon vanilla

Pour boiling water over the cocoa, pouring slowly and stirring mixture until it is the consistency of cake batter. Beat egg yolks until thick and lemon colored. Cream butter and sugar well. Add beaten egg yolks and chocolate mixture. Add soda to milk; add half of milk, then half of flour, alternately. Add vanilla; fold in beaten egg whites. Bake in two rectangular pans 20 minutes at 350°; ice cake with your favorite icing, while the cake is still warm. This makes a large cake.

Bonnie Davis, Phoenix

CHOCOLATE ICING

2 cups sugar
1/2 cup milk
1/2 cup nuts, grated

3 squares unsweetened chocolate
1/2 teaspoon salt
1 teaspoon vanilla

Mix all ingredients, except grated nuts. Put the mixture over low heat and stir until melted. Let it come to an all-over boil and boil 1 minute. Add vanilla and beat well. Start spreading the icing on cake while it is very soft. Sprinkle nuts between layers and on top of the cake.

Bonnie Davis
Tempe, AZ

LEMON SURPRISE BUNDT CAKE

1 package lemon supreme cake mix
1/2 cup sugar
3/4 cup Wesson oil
1 cup apricot juice
4 eggs

Topping for cake:

2 cups powdered sugar
Lemon juice to taste
Apricot juice to taste

Place all but the eggs in a bowl. Mix until well blended. Add the eggs one at a time, stirring until each egg is well blended. Put this batter in a Bundt pan which has been buttered well and floured. Bake at 325° for 40 minutes in oven. When done, leave in the pan for 5 minutes, then turn onto a cake rack. Mix powdered sugar, lemon juice and just enough apricot juice to make a thin mix to drizzle over the cake.

Mary Racich Bicker, Louisville, Kentucky

APPLE SAUCE CAKE

1/2 cup shortening (butter)
1 cup sugar
1-1/2 cups applesauce
2 cups flour, sifted with
2 level teaspoons soda
1/2 teaspoon allspice
1 teaspoon cinnamon
1 teaspoon cloves
1 cup raisins
Dates, candied fruit, or watermelon preserves, as preferred

Cream shortening and sugar. Add applesauce and flour. Mix well and then add other ingredients. Put wax paper in pan and bake in slow oven 350° for 1 hour. Test with toothpick. For higher altitudes, baking may take longer. When finished, sprinkle with powdered sugar and candied cherries. (Submitted in memory of my sister, Ethel Hawkins)

Eva Shaw Lee

RED VELVET LAYER CAKE & ICING

2-1/2 cups all-purpose flour
1-1/2 cups sugar
2 teaspoons cocoa
1 teaspoon soda
1 teaspoon salt
2 whole eggs
2 cups salad oil (Wesson)
1 cup buttermilk
2 ounces (1/4 cup) red food coloring
1 teaspoon vinegar
1 teaspoon vanilla

Place all dry ingredients in mixing bowl. Blend eggs with fork. Add oil and blend again. Add all to dry ingredients and mix until smooth with wire whip or electric mixer on medium speed. Add and blend the buttermilk. Pour equally into 3 layer cake pans (8" size 1" deep) that have been greased and floured. Bake at 350° for 30 minutes. Cool slightly and remove from pans. Ice with the following:

8 ounces cream cheese (room temperature)
1 box (1 pound) powdered sugar
1/4 pound (1 stick) oleo or butter
1 teaspoon vanilla extract
1 cup (4 ounces) chopped pecans

Mix until light and fluffy and ice the cake.

Wanda Cluff

APPLE CAKE

4 cups apples, chopped
2 cups sugar
2 cups flour
2 eggs
2 teaspoons baking soda
2 teaspoons cinnamon
1 teaspoon cloves
2 teaspoons vanilla
1/2 teaspoon salt
1 package nuts, chopped
1/2 cup oil or butter

Beat eggs slightly; add to the sugar and oil. Sift the flour, soda, salt and spices; add to the egg mixture. Stir in the apples and nuts. Bake in 350° oven for 45 minutes.

Marcelina Jampi

7-UP POUND CAKE

2 sticks margarine
1/2 cup shortening
3 cups sugar
5 eggs
3 cups flour
7 ounces of 7-UP
1 teaspoon vanilla, or lemon juice

Mix everything in bowl together and beat until well blended. Pour in a greased floured tube pan. Bake at 350° for 1 hour and 20 minutes. Let cool in pan at least 20 minutes before removing.

Mary Hufnagel, Tucson, Arizona

SPONGE CAKE

6 eggs
1-1/4 cups sugar
1/4 teaspoon salt
Juice from 1 orange, about 1/3 cup)
1-1/4 cups flour
1 teaspoon vanilla

Beat egg yolks until lemon colored. Add sugar and beat. Add orange juice and beat until creamy. Add beaten egg whites. Add flour and salt. Add vanilla. Place in cold oven. Set oven at moderate heat and turn on lower element only. Bake 45 minutes. Turn upside down to cool.

Laura M. Williams

LEMON CHEESE CAKE

1/4 cup lemon juice
4 packages (3 ounces each) cream cheese
2 eggs, beaten
3/4 cup granulated sugar

Combine lemon juice and cream cheese. Cream well. Add beaten eggs and sugar. Beat until fluffy. Pour into vanilla wafer crust (See below). Bake at 350° for 15 to 20 minutes. Remove from oven; cool 5 minutes.

VANILLA WAFER CRUST (For Lemon Cheese Cake)

1 cup vanilla wafer crumbs, (about 30)	1 tablespoon granulated sugar
2 tablespoons butter, melted	1 tablespoon lemon juice
	Pinch of salt

Mix above ingredients, reserving a few crumbs for top. Press crumb mixture evenly and firmly on bottom and sides of 8-inch pie pan. Pour in filling. Bake as directed above.

TOPPING

1 tablespoon sugar
1 tablespoon grated lemon rind
1 cup sour cream

Mix together. Spread over pie. Return to oven and bake 10 minutes. Chill at least 5 hours before serving. Decorate top with lemon slices and cookie mixture, if desired.

Olga Svob Dugan, Downey, California

"Rev. Sabino Gonzalez built the Mexican Methodist Church of amunition boxes--hence the name The Powder Box Church."

OATMEAL CAKE

1 cup quick rolled oats
1-1/4 cups boiling water
1 cup brown sugar
1 cup white sugar
1/2 cup shortening

1-1/2 cups flour
1 teaspoon cinnamon
1 teaspoon soda
2 eggs, beaten
  separately

Combine and let stand the oats and boiling water. To the sugar and the shortening add egg yolks and oatmeal mixture. Sift together the flour, cinnamon and soda. Add to first mixture. Beat egg whites until stiff and fold in. Pour into greased and floured pan. Bake at 350° till done. (See recipe for frosting below.)

FROSTING FOR OATMEAL CAKE

3/4 cup brown sugar
1/3 cup butter
1/4 cup milk

1/2 cup coconut,
  shredded
1/2 cup nuts, chopped

Stir together, but do not cook. Pour on the cake while hot and place under broiler until brown.
                                               Marilyn Rome

COCONUT POUND CAKE

6 eggs, separated
1 cup margarine
1/2 cup shortening
3 cups sugar
1/2 teaspoon almond extract
1 teaspoon vanilla

1/2 teaspoon salt
3 cups flour, sifted
1 cup milk
2 cups coconut,
  shredded

Let eggs warm at room temperature and separate. Put yolks in bowl with shortening. Gradually add sugar, then extracts and salt. Mix well. Mix in flour and milk alternately. Add coconut and beat until blended. Beat egg whites until stiff peaks form and add to mixture. Bake in 10-inch tube pan at 300° 2 hours. I also add 1 tablespoon more of flour. This cake serves 20 people.
                                               Phyllis Miller

"Indians were mining in the area 300 years before Columbus came to the New World. They found such treasures as azurite, turquoise, and copper ore."

RHUBARB CAKE

1 stick (1/2 cup) margarine
1-1/2 cups brown sugar, packed
1 egg, beaten
2 cups flour
1 teaspoon salt
1 teaspoon soda

1 cup buttermilk
1 teaspoon vanilla
1-1/2 cups raw rhubarb, cut fine
1/2 cup chopped nuts, if desired

Cream together margarine and sugar; add eggs and blend. Sift together flour and soda. Add flour and liquids alternately, mixing well. Fold rhubarb into mixture. Bake in 9 x 13-inch pan at 350° for 30 to 35 minutes. Sprinkle topping over dough. (See recipe below)

TOPPING FOR RHUBARB CAKE: Mix sugar with cinnamon; sprinkle.

Kathleen Berg

SERGUTEN (VERY GOOD) CRUMB CAKE

2-1/4 cups brown sugar
3/4 cup butter or oleo
3 cups flour
1 teaspoon soda
1 teaspoon cinnamon

1/2 teaspoon cloves
1/2 teaspoon allspice
1 cup buttermilk
1 egg, beaten
1 cup raisins

Mix brown sugar, oleo and flour thoroughly. Take out 1-2/3 cups of this mixture and save for topping. Then to the remaining add soda, the spices, buttermilk and egg. Mix well, then add the raisins that have been floured lightly. Pour into large pan that has been greased and floured. Put the 1-2/3 cups crumbs on top, spreading them evenly. Bake at 375° until done. This recipe was handed down to me from my German mother.

Verna Blair

DATE CHEWS

2 eggs
1/2 cup sugar
1 teaspoon vanilla
1/2 cup flour, sifted

1/2 teaspoon baking powder
1/2 teaspoon salt
1 cup nuts, coarsely chopped
1-1/2 cup dates, snipped

Beat eggs till thick and foamy; add sugar and vanilla. Sift flour with baking powder and salt. Fold in nuts and dates. Spread in a well-greased and floured 8-inch square pan. Bake in a slow oven 325° for 35 to 40 minutes. Cut in squares while warm. Cool, remove from pan and roll in powdered sugar. Makes 16 squares of 2-inch cuttings.

Ruth Cantrell

CHEESE CAKE

Crust:
    18 zwieback biscuits rolled into fine crumbs
    3 tablespoons butter, or margarine
    1 tablespoon sugar

Pre-heat oven to 300° and maintain this temperature while baking cake. Blend crumbs, butter and sugar. Press into bottom and sides of buttered 9-inch cake pan. Bake 5 minutes and let cool.

Filling:
    1 pound soft cream cheese
    1/2 cup sugar
    1/8 teaspoon cinnamon
    1/2 teaspoon vanilla
    1 tablespoon lemon juice
    2 eggs, separated

Blend cheese and sugar, cinnamon, vanilla and lemon juice. Beat in yolks one at a time. Fold in stiffly beaten egg whites. Pour mixture on top of crumb crust when it is cool. Bake at 300° for 45 minutes.

Topping:
    1 cup sour cream
    1 tablespoon sugar
    1 teaspoon vanilla

Blend sour cream with sugar and vanilla. Spread on baked cake, then bake for 10 more minutes. Cool and chill before serving.

                              Frances Driussi, Rialto, California

POTATO CAKE

1 cup butter
2 cups sugar
1 cup mashed potatoes
4 egg yolks
1/2 cup buttermilk with
    1/2 teaspoon soda
2 cups flour

1/2 teaspoon baking powder
1/4 cup cocoa
1 teaspoon cinnamon
1 teaspoon nutmeg
1 teaspoon cloves
1 teaspoon vanilla
4 egg whites

Mix well the butter, sugar, mashed potatoes, egg yolks, buttermilk and soda. Add flour which has been sifted with baking powder, cocoa and spices. Add vanilla. Fold in stiffly beaten egg whites. Bake in angel food cake pan which has been greased and floured. Bake at 350° for about 1 hour.
                                                  Bertha Hughes

STRAWBERRY ORANGE CHIFFON CAKE

6 eggs, separated
1 tablespoon orange peel, grated
1/2 cup orange juice
1-1/4 cups flour
1-1/2 cups sugar
1/4 teaspoon salt
1 teaspoon cream of tartar
2 cups fresh strawberries
1-1/2 cups whipping cream

Beat the egg yolks for 5 minutes, until lemon color; add grated orange peel, orange juice; beat until thick. Combine flour with 1/3 cup of the sugar and set aside. Gradually add 2/3 cup sugar and salt to the egg mixture, beating constantly. Sift flour mixture a little at a time over the egg mixture, folding just until blended; wash beaters. Beat the egg whites until soft peaks form and add cream of tartar to the egg whites before beating. Gradually add 1/2 cup sugar and beat until whites form stiff peaks. Lighten egg yolk mixture with about 2 tablespoons of egg white mixture, then fold whites into egg yolk mixture until blended. Pour into ungreased 10-inch tube pan. Bake in 325° oven for 55 minutes; remove from oven and cool on cake rack. When cool, split cake into three layers; slice strawberries; whip the cream; put strawberries and whipped cream between layers, saving a few of the strawberries for trim on top.   Delores Santillan

CHEESE CAKE

Crust: 1 package zwieback   Filling: 1 pound cream cheese
         2 tablespoons sugar   Pinch of salt
         2 tablespoons butter   1/4 cup flour
                                            1 cup sugar
                                            1 teaspoon vanilla
                                            4 eggs, separated
                                            1 cup milk

Roll zwieback into crumbs; add butter and sugar and rub until well blended. Put half of mixture in bottom of lightly greased pan and press down evenly all around. Cream sugar with cheese; add flour, salt, vanilla and beaten egg yolks. Mix well and add milk. Fold in beaten egg whites. Pour into pan on top of crumbs. Pour remaining half of crumbs on top. Bake in slow oven 325° for 1 hour or more until no depression is left when touched in center with finger. Use pan 12x18 size.
                                                          Mary Vojnic

CLEOPATRA HILL PRUNE CAKE

2 cups sugar
1 cup shortening
1/2 teaspoon salt
4 eggs
6 teaspoons sour milk
1/2 teaspoon cloves
2 teaspoons soda
1 teaspoon baking powder

2 cups cooked prunes, diced
3 cups flour, sifted
1 cup nuts
2 teaspoons cinnamon
1 teaspoon nutmeg
1/2 teaspoon orange rind, grated
1/2 teaspoon lemon juice

Cream sugar and shortening. Add eggs and cream well. Sift all dry ingredients together, except soda which is added to the prunes and sour milk until mixture is foamy. To creamed mixture add the flour and prune mixture, stirring well after each addition. Add lemon juice, nuts and orange rind. Bake in large oblong cake pan at 350° for 1 hour, or until toothpick comes out clean. When cake is thoroughly cooled, frost with cream cheese frosting below:

CREAM CHEESE FROSTING

1 package (8-ounce) Philadelphia cream cheese
3 cups confectioners sugar
Butter, enough to soften
Milk, a small amount
1 teaspoon vanilla

Cream the sugar with the cream cheese, adding butter to soften; then add the milk and vanilla to complete the frosting mixture.

Connie Stevenson

CANADIAN SHORTBREAD

1 cup soft butter or margarine
1/2 cup powdered sugar
1/4 cup cornstarch
1-1/2 cup flour

Preheat oven to 325°. Sift dry ingredients over butter in a bowl. Beat at low speed until blended. Then beat at high speed until it resembles whipped cream. Drop by spoonfuls on ungreased cooky sheet. Bake about 15 minutes. These will keep well, if you hide them!

Winifred S. Foster

WHITE FRUIT CAKE

5 eggs
1/2 pound oleo, melted
1 cup sugar
1/2 cup orange juice
1 cup coconut
1 pound fruit cake mix
1 small glass of jelly
2 cups flour
1 teaspoon each of baking powder, cloves, allspice, cinnamon
1/2 pound dates, cut up
1-1/2 cups walnuts

Beat eggs, add sugar, cooled oleo, orange juice and jelly; blend well. Add sifted dry ingredients. Mix well. Add fruit, nuts and coconut. This makes a large angel food pan size cake, or two loaf size pans. Grease and flour pan. Bake at 250° for several hours; test with a toothpick. Let cool in pans 30 minutes before removing. When cake is cool, wrap in foil. Keeps for weeks in refrigerator, or is good the day you bake it.   Helen Sullivan, Winslow, Arizona

CARAWAY CAKE

Not quite 1/4 pound butter
3/4 cup sugar
1 teaspoon salt
1 teaspoon soda
1 teaspoon baking powder
2 eggs
1 cup buttermilk
2-1/2 cups flour
1 to 2 tablespoons caraway seed

Cream butter and sugar. Add eggs. Add soda to buttermilk and combine with creamed mixture. Add baking powder and flour and fold (do not beat!). Distribute and fold in caraway seeds. Bake in 325° oven in greased, floured, loaf pan for 45 minutes to 1 hour.   Katie Sullivan

RAISIN SPICE POUND CAKE

1 package spice cake mix
1 package (small) vanilla instant pudding
1/2 cup Wesson or Mazola oil
1 cup water
4 eggs
1 cup raisins
1 cup powdered sugar
2 tablespoons milk

Blend all ingredients except powdered sugar and milk. Beat 2 minutes. Pour into greased and floured Bundt pan. Bake 45 minutes to 1 hour at 350° and cool for 1/2 hour. Remove from pan. Make a glaze of the powdered sugar and milk. Drizzle over cake. Garnish with cherries, nuts, or strawberries.

Fay Horton

"COUSIN JACK" COOKIES

3 cups flour
1 cup brown sugar
1 cup shortening
1 cup seedless raisins
1/4 teaspoon salt

1/4 teaspoon nutmeg
2-1/2 teaspoons baking powder
1 teaspoon vanilla
2/3 cup milk
1 egg

Sift flour, salt, baking powder and nutmeg together. Work in shortening as for pie crust. Add sugar and raisins. Beat together egg, milk, and vanilla. Stir in dry ingredients. Roll about 1/4-inch thick. Cut with cookie cutter. Bake for about 10 minutes in 400° oven or until golden brown.

Irma Killough

HERMIT'S COOKIES

6 tablespoons shortening
1 cup brown sugar
1 egg, beaten
1-1/2 cups flour, sifted
2 teaspoons baking powder

1 teaspoon cloves
1 teaspoon allspice
1 teaspoon cinnamon
1/4 teaspoon salt
1 cup raisins and walnuts, chopped

Cream shortening and sugar together and add egg. Sift together dry ingredients. Add to creamed mixture. Mix well. Add raisins and nuts. Drop from spoon on greased cookie sheet. Bake at 375° for 12 minutes.

Drucilla Catlin

YUMMY BARS

1 package German chocolate cake mix
3/4 cup butter, melted
2/3 cup evaporated milk

1 package (6-ounce) chocolate chips
1 cup pecans, or walnuts
10 caramels, melted in milk

Mix cake mix with melted butter and 1/3 cup of evaporated milk. Put half of mixture in 9x13-inch pan and bake at 350° for 6 minutes; remove from oven; add chocolate chips, nuts and caramel mixture which has been prepared by melting the caramels in the other 1/3 cup of milk by the time first mixture is out of the first baking period. Then bake again 15 to 20 minutes at 350° but do not cut until cool. "It's very rich, so cut in 1 or 1-1/2 inch squares."

Maureen Kennedy

CRANBERRY KITCHEN COOKIES

1/2 cup butter, or margarine
1 cup granulated sugar
3/4 cup firmly packed brown sugar
1 egg
1/4 cup milk
2 tablespoons orange juice

3 cups all-purpose flour
1 teaspoon baking powder
1/4 teaspoon baking soda
1/2 teaspoon salt
1 cup nuts, chopped
2-1/2 cups fresh cranberries, coarsely chopped

Preheat oven to 375° while creaming butter and sugars together. Beat in the egg, then the milk and orange juice. Sift flour, baking powder, baking soda and salt together. Add to creamed mixture and blend well. Stir in chopped nuts and cranberries. Drop by teaspoonfuls onto greased baking sheets. Bake in moderate oven 375° for 10 to 15 minutes, or until browned.
Geneva Schwalm

ORANGE SUGAR COOKIES

2/3 cup butter (no substitute)
1-1/4 cups sugar
2 eggs
3 cups flour

1/2 teaspoon salt
2 teaspoons baking powder
1 tablespoon orange juice
Rind of 1 orange

Mix in usual way. Roll thin and cut in desired shapes. Sprinkle with sugar before baking or frost cookies afterward. Bake in 350° oven for about 8 minutes until lightly browned. Use an ungreased cookie sheet. This is my favorite for the holidays.
Irene McDonald

G-O-O-D COOKIES

1 cup Wesson oil
1 cup butter (I use Imperial margarine)
1 cup brown sugar
1 cup white sugar
1 egg, beaten
1 cup crushed corn flakes

1 cup oatmeal
1/2 cup nuts, chopped
1 teaspoon salt
1 teaspoon vanilla
1 teaspoon soda
3-1/2 cups flour

Drop 1 teaspoon of mixture on cookie sheet. Pat down with bottom of a glass dipped in sugar. Bake at 375° for 12 minutes or until light brown. Makes about 100 cookies. Dough may be stored in refrigerator and baked as needed.
Bernice Jackson

COOKIE COOLERS

1 box powdered sugar
1 box (12-ounce) vanilla wafers
1 cup nuts, chopped
1 stick margarine

1 can (6-ounce) orange
   juice, thawed
1 teaspoon vanilla

Mix well the sugar, crushed wafers, nuts and margarine; add the orange juice and vanilla. Mix well and chill at least 1 hour. Shape into small balls and roll in fine coconut. Makes 12 dozen small cookies.

Rosella Kennedy

CHOCOLATE HALFWAY BARS

1 cup flour
1/2 teaspoon salt
1/8 teaspoon baking powder
1/2 teaspoon baking soda
1/2 cup Crisco
1/4 cup granulated sugar

3/4 cup brown sugar
1 egg, separated
1-1/2 teaspoons water
1/2 teaspoon vanilla
1 package (6 ounces)
   chocolate chips

Grease 8x12 pan. Mix Crisco with white sugar and 1/4 cup of the brown sugar until light and fluffy. Add egg yolk, water and vanilla. Mix flour, salt, soda and baking powder. Pat into pan, top with chips. Beat egg white until stiff, add 1/2 cup brown sugar to egg white and beat again until very stiff. When stiff, spread over chips. Bake at 375° for 25 minutes. Cool in pan. Recipe makes 32 bars.

Thelma K. Ferrell

PUMPKIN SPICE COOKIES

1-3/4 cups all purpose flour
1/2 teaspoon salt
1 teaspoon cinnamon
1/2 teaspoon nutmeg
1/2 teaspoon ginger
1/2 teaspoon cloves

1 cup seeded raisins
1 cup canned pumpkin
1 teaspoon soda
1/2 cup shortening
1 cup sugar
1 egg

Bring raisins to boil in a little water to plump them nicely. Sift together first 6 ingredients. Combine pumpkin with soda. Mix shortening and sugar until creamy. Add egg and mix well. Mix in flour alternately with pumpkin. Now stir in the cooled raisins. Drop by teaspoon about 2 inches apart on greased cooky sheet. Bake at 375° about 20 minutes.

Bertha Hughes

COCKTAIL COOKIES

1/2 cup flour
1/4 cup butter
1 jar processed bacon-and-cheese spread

Shape into neat roll; wrap in waxed paper and refrigerate. When firm, slice as for cookies. Bake at 400° for 10 minutes. (No need to grease the pan.)
Frankie Vincent

TOM THUMB COOKIE BARS

1/2 cup Spry
1/2 teaspoon salt
1-1/2 cups brown sugar, firmly packed
1 cup flour, sifted
1 teaspoon vanilla
2 eggs, well beaten
2 tablespoons flour
1/2 teaspoon baking powder
1-1/2 cups shredded coconut
1 cup nuts, coarsely cut

Combine spry and salt. Add 1/2 cup of the brown sugar and cream this thoroughly. Add the flour and blend. Grease 8"x12" pan with spry and dust with flour. Put above mixture in pan and bake in moderately slow oven 325° for 15 minutes or until delicately browned. Add remaining cup brown sugar and vanilla to beaten eggs that are thick and foamy. Then add 2 tablespoons flour, baking powder, coconut and nuts; blend. Spread over baked mixture; return to oven same temperature and bake 25 minutes. Cool and cut in small rectangles. Makes 3 dozen bars.
Virginia Mick

GRANDMOTHER'S COOKIES

2 cups sugar
2 eggs
1 cup butter
1 cup sour cream
1 teaspoon nutmeg
Flour enough to make a stiff dough

Roll dough until one inch thick. Cut and bake in medium hot oven until brown.
Fae K. Bean, Clarkdale, Arizona

APPLE SAUCE COOKIES

3/4 cup shortening
1 cup brown sugar
1 egg, beaten
1/2 cup apple sauce
2-1/4 cups sifted flour
1/2 teaspoon soda
1/2 teaspoon salt

3/4 teaspoon cinnamon
1/4 teaspoon cloves
1 cup raisins
1/2 cup nuts, chopped
1/2 cup candied fruits, if desired

Cream sugar and shortening; add egg and apple sauce. Mix soda, salt and spices together with the flour. Mix all well; add raisins and nuts. Drop by teaspoon on greased cookie sheet. Pre-heat oven to 375° and bake the cookies for 10 to 12 minutes. Recipe makes 4 dozen cookies. For Christmas cookies, add 1/2 cup candied fruit and 1/2 cup raisins. These cookies are rich and moist; they keep well.   Elizabeth Nihell

ICEBOX COOKIES

3 eggs
1/2 cup shortening
2 cups flour
1/2 cup brown sugar

1 teaspoon baking powder
1/4 teaspoon salt
1/2 teaspoon soda
1/2 teaspoon cinnamon
1/2 cup nuts

Cream shortening and sugar. Add eggs. Sift flour, baking powder, salt, soda, cinnamon, together and add to the first mixture. Bake at 325° for 10 minutes. "This recipe is from my Mary's cookbook!"
Val Harris, Berkeley, California

THUMB PRINTS

1 cup sugar
1 cup butter, or margarine
2 egg yolks
1 teaspoon vanilla

2 cups sifted flour
1 cup nuts, or more
Maraschino cherries

Cream sugar, butter and egg yolks. Mix and roll into small balls. Roll into egg whites that have been slightly beaten. Then roll in chopped nuts. Grease cookie sheet a little. Bake at 375° for 5 to 8 minutes. Take out of oven; make a thumb print in each cookie. Put a half cherry in each. Return to oven and bake about 3 minutes longer, or until light brown. These are worth the little extra work; they are delicious.
Margaret Smull

GINGER CHRISTMAS COOKIES—Good at any time!

1 cup sugar	1/2 teaspoon cloves
1 cup shortening	1 teaspoon nutmeg
1 cup molasses	1 teaspoon cinnamon
1 egg, beaten	1 teaspoon ginger
1 teaspoon soda in 1/2 cup hot water	5 cups flour (or more)

Cream shortening; add sugar gradually, then molasses and egg. Combine soda and hot water and add to the first mixture. Stir in flour, sifted with salt and spices. Blend thoroughly. Chill in refrigerator several hours. Roll out on well floured board. If the dough is too soft to cut figures, add more flour. Bake in a moderate oven 8 to 10 minutes or slower. I cut my figures from children's coloring books, etc. These cookies seem to stay soft longer than most.   Ruth Corlett

MEXICAN WEDDING RING COOKIES

1/2 cup sugar	1 cup nuts
1 cup oleo	1/2 teaspoon vanilla
Pinch of salt	A few drops of green
2 cups flour	food coloring

This is a good Christmas cookie. Mix all ingredients. Form into small balls and bake at 350° until done, about 12 to 15 minutes. When cool roll in powdered sugar.   Sally Grigg Crawford, Bishop, California

CATHEDRAL WINDOWS

1 package (6-ounce) chocolate chips	1-1/2 cups powdered sugar
1 cube margarine	1 package small colored marshmallows
1 egg, well beaten	1/2 cup nuts, chopped

Melt together in double boiler, without stirring, the chocolate chips and margarine. Pour into bowl containing egg. Cool slightly. Stir in powdered sugar, marshmallows and nuts. Pour mixture on a board covered with powdered sugar and coconut. Divide into two parts. Roll into logs, coating with powdered sugar and coconut. Wrap in wax paper and put in refrigerator overnight or for several hours. Slice.

Marilyn Rome

SOUR CREAM COOKIES

1 cup sugar
2 eggs
1 teaspoon soda
1/2 teaspoon cloves
1 cup raisins
1 teaspoon cinnamon

Pinch of salt
1 cup sour cream
2 cups flour
1 cup nuts
Candied fruit,
as desired

Dissolve soda in sour cream. Beat eggs, add sugar, then beat well. Add cream, flour, salt and spices. Add nuts and raisins (add candied fruit for holiday cookies). Drop on greased pan and bake in hot oven about 7 minutes.   Laura M. Williams

AUNT MARY'S COOKIES

2 cups sugar
1/2 cup butter
1/2 cup lard
1 cup cold water
2 eggs
1 teaspoon soda
2 teaspoons cream of tartar
1/4 teaspoon salt
Flavoring as desired
Flour enough to make a soft dough

This recipe from a former nurse in Jerome (1920-1930) has been thought to be well over 100 years old and has been used by Jerome pioneers far and near. The former nurse who sent us the recipe is now residing in the Arizona Pioneers Home at Prescott. She gives simple direction indeed— "Use enough flour to make a soft dough."   Hazel B. Logan

YUGOSLAVIAN KUGLOV

1 pound margarine
1 pound powdered sugar
6 large eggs

1 tablespoon vanilla
3 cups unsifted flour
Raisins, as desired

Cream margarine; add powdered sugar and eggs; beat well. Add flour a little at a time. Add vanilla and beat well. Put in well greased tube pan and bake at 400° for 1 hour.   Dorothy Vladich

DESSERTS & PASTRIES

JELLO PIE DESSERT

1 package cherry jello
1/2 cup hot water
1/4 cup lemon juice
1/4 cup sugar

1 small can Pet milk, chilled
1 small can crushed pineapple
Graham cracker pie crust

Mix jello, hot water, lemon juice and sugar and let stand while whipping Pet milk. Add whipped milk to the first mixture and beat. Pour in the pineapple that has been drained. Pour into graham cracker pie crust.

Ethel Devine

DATE PUDDING

1 pound dates, pitted
1 cup nuts, chopped
1/2 cup sugar or honey
6 tablespoons flour
2-1/4 teaspoons baking powder
4 eggs

Mix thoroughly. Bake slowly at 300° for 1-1/2 hours. This is a very old recipe, about 1890, from my grandmother. Arizona pioneer women originated it to utilize the local crops in Phoenix and Tempe.

Frankie Vincent

CARROT PUDDING

1 cup carrots, grated
1 cup potatoes, grated
1 cup flour
1 cup sugar
1 cup raisins
1 cup nuts, chopped
2 tablespoons butter, melted

1/2 teaspoon soda
1/2 teaspoon salt
1/2 teaspoon cloves
1/2 teaspoon cinnamon
1/2 teaspoon nutmeg
1/2 teaspoon vanilla

Mix all ingredients and cook in double boiler for 4 hours. Serve either warm or cold with Brown Sauce (Recipe below).

BROWN SAUCE FOR CARROT PUDDING

1 cup brown sugar
2 tablespoons flour
1 cup boiling water
1 tablespoon butter

Bourbon or rum, for
flavoring as desired
Vanilla, if desired

Mix flour and sugar; add boiling water and cook until thickened. Remove, cool, add flavoring. This is an old recipe traditionally used in our family at Thanksgiving and Christmas. It is one of the old pioneer recipes, "cup-to-cup." It came from my mother's family, the Allens, who arrived in Verde Valley in 1874 from Kansas. There were five wagons in this group, and after arriving in Camp Verde, they began the little community of Cherry. Ruth Davis

DATE NUT PIE

1 egg
3/4 cup sugar
1/2 cup flour
1 teaspoon baking powder
1/4 teaspoon salt

1 teaspoon vanilla
1 cup apples, cubed
1/3 cup pecans, chopped
10 dates, cut up
Whipped cream or van-
    illa ice cream

Beat egg and sugar together; add flour, baking powder, salt and the vanilla; then add the apples, pecans and dates. Pour into lightly greased 9 or 10-inch pie plate and bake at 325 to 350° for 30 minutes. This recipe makes 1 pie. Ruth Sullivan

CHESS PIE

1/2 cup Wesson butter oil
1 cup sugar
2 tablespoons flour
1 cup raisins
1 cup walnuts, chopped
3 eggs, well beaten
1 teaspoon vanilla

Soak raisins in hot water and set aside. Stir well the butter oil, sugar, and flour. Drain raisins and add walnuts, eggs and vanilla. Combine all and put into unbaked pie crust shell to bake at 350° for 40 minutes. Recipe by pioneer who came to Jerome in 1903 and was reared here; a sister of Tony Stadelman. "This recipe is great, has traveled all over the world and will keep as long as a fruit cake." Mary Fischer Matheny

BREAD PUDDING

2 cups milk
1/3 cup butter
4 cups coarse bread crumbs
1/2 cup plus 1 tablespoon sugar
2 eggs, slightly beaten
1/4 teaspoon salt
1/2 cup raisins
1 teaspoon cinnamon
1/4 teaspoon nutmeg,
Vanilla, as desired

Scald milk and remove from heat. Melt butter in the milk and then pour mixture over bread crumbs. Add rest of ingredients. Pour into buttered casserole and bake at 350° for 40 to 45 minutes, or until silver knife comes out clean. For a fancy dessert make a hard sauce to go with it (See recipe below) and serve warm. Serves 6 or 7 people.
Hard Sauce:
Cream margarine or butter; add the milk and powdered sugar until it looks like a thick butter frosting. Flavor with the vanilla. Recipe makes about 1 cup, just enough to dab on each portion of the pudding. "A great favorite in my native Jerome"
Neda Blazina Mercier, Albuquerque, N.M.

HARD SAUCE FOR BREAD PUDDING

1/2 cup butter, or margarine
1-1/2 cups powdered sugar
2 teaspoons vanilla

WALNUT PUMPKIN PUDDING — STEAMED

1 cup walnuts, chopped
1/2 cup shortening,
 half butter
1 cup brown sugar, packed
1/4 cup granulated sugar
1/2 teaspoon each of
 cinnamon, nutmeg and ginger
1-1/2 teaspoons salt

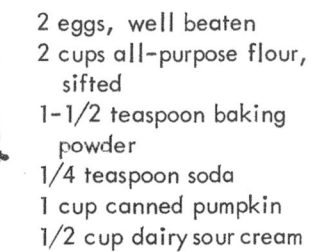

2 eggs, well beaten
2 cups all-purpose flour,
 sifted
1-1/2 teaspoon baking
 powder
1/4 teaspoon soda
1 cup canned pumpkin
1/2 cup dairy sour cream

Cream shortening, brown and white sugar, and spices until light and fluffy. Beat in eggs; stir in walnuts. Resift flour with baking powder, soda and salt. Add to creamed mixture alternately with pumpkin and sour cream. Turn into a well greased 1-1/2 or 2-quart mold. Cover tightly. Set mold in pan of hot water half way up. Replenish water, if necessary during steaming. Cover pan and cook about 2 hours. Let stand 5 minutes before removing. (See recipe for sauce below)

BRANDY WHIPPED CREAM SAUCE

1 egg
1/3 cup butter, melted
1-1/2 cups powdered sugar, sifted

1 tablespoon brandy extract
Pinch of salt
1 cup whipping cream

Beat the egg until light and fluffy. Beat in the butter, powdered sugar, salt and extract. Beat the whipping cream until stiff. Gently fold in the first mixture. Cover and chill until ready to serve. Stir before spooning onto pudding.   Louise Heyer

PUMPKIN PIE

1-1/2 cups cooked pumpkin
1 cup milk
1 cup sugar
1/4 teaspoon salt

1 tablespoon butter, melted
1/4 teaspoon nutmeg
1/2 teaspoon cinnamon
2 eggs (slightly beaten)

This recipe makes 1 pie and is so simple—making a foolproof and very delicious pie everytime!—so I thought it might be worthwhile to pass it along, even though it is such a common thing. Combine the above ingredients. Mix well and pour into pastry-lined pie dish. Bake at 325° for about 1-1/2 hours. Test periodically with a dry knife after 1-1/4 hours of baking. When the knife comes out clean, the pie is done. Delicious with whipped cream that has had some powdered sugar added before whipping.   Karen Brown

NEW ENGLAND SQUASH PIE

1-3/4 cups mashed squash (Hubbard)
1 teaspoon salt
1-1/2 cups milk
3 eggs
1 cup sugar

1 teaspoon cinnamon
1/2 teaspoon nutmeg
1/2 teaspoon ginger
1 tablespoon melted butter

Combine ingredients and pour into pastry-lined 9-inch pie pan and bake at 425° (hot oven) for 45 to 55 minutes.   Laura Bowman

PIE CRUST

1/3 cup Crisco
1/2 teaspoon salt
1 cup flour
3 to 4 tablespoons cold water

Mix shortening, salt and flour with fork until mixture is the size of small peas. Sprinkle cold water, a tablespoon at a time, while tossing and stirring lightly with fork. Add water until dough is just moist enough to hold together. Form into a ball and roll out 1 inch larger than your pan. Fold pastry in half or roll in large rolls and place on pan and unfold and fit loosely in pan, gently patting out any air pockets.
                Laura Bowman

STRAWBERRY PIE

2 boxes strawberries
3/4 cup water
3 tablespoons cornstarch
1 cup sugar
1 teaspoon lemon juice
1/4 teaspoon red food coloring

Cook one box of the berries and thicken with the remaining ingredients. Put the uncooked berries in baked shell. Pour the partly cooled strawberry mixture over them. Cover with whipped cream.
                Margaret Smull

VINEGAR PIE

1 cup sugar
2 eggs, beaten
2 tablespoons vinegar
1/2 teaspoon lemon extract

1 cup water
2 tablespoons flour, or cornstarch
Small lump of butter
1 baked pie shell

Cook sugar, eggs, vinegar, water and flour in a double boiler until thick and smooth, stirring occasionally. Just before removing from heat stir in butter and lemon extract. Pour into baked pie shell. Cool and top with meringue or whipped cream. This is an extremely old recipe originating from my European ancestors. Phyllis Miller

SUET PUDDING WITH HARD SAUCE

1 cup suet, chopped fine
3/4 cup sugar
1/2 cup molasses
1/2 teaspoon baking soda, dissolved in 1/2 cup water
1 egg
2 cups milk

3 cups flour
1 package seeded raisins
1 teaspoon cinnamon
1/2 teaspoon cloves
1/2 teaspoon nutmeg
1/2 teaspoon allspice

Mix and tie in dish towel. Leave room for swelling. Put plate in kettle to prevent pudding from sticking to bottom. Bring water to boil. Put pudding in kettle and boil for 2 hours. Serve with hard sauce. Pudding can be reheated and served with the sauce. Make hard sauce by recipe below. This was served by my mother, Mrs. Melena Metzler, and the recipe came from England.

Ethel Mortensen, Oxnard, California

HARD SAUCE FOR SUET PUDDING:

1 egg
Powdered sugar, as needed
Butter, as needed
Rum flavoring

"The first claim was filed in 1876 by two prospectors, Angus McKinnon and M. A. Ruffner. They proceeded to dig a 45' shaft with their primitive equipment."

ENGLISH APPLE PIE

Apples, as needed
Spices to taste
1 cup flour
1/2 cup butter
1/2 cup brown sugar

Slice apples thin and place in deep pie dish or other pan or dish. Sugar and spice as for any other pie. Add a little flour. Then mix remaining flour with butter and brown sugar-with knives till it crumbles. Sprinkle on top of apples and bake in moderate oven till apples are tender, 30 to 40 minutes. Geraldine Thomas

HATTIE'S DELIGHT, A PEACH DESSERT

1/4 cup sugar
2 eggs, separated
3 tablespoons Crisco
1 lemon, both rind and juice
1 cup flour
1/2 cup milk
3 teaspoons baking powder
1/2 teaspoon salt
8 to 10 large peaches

Blend sugar, egg yolks and Crisco in a few fast stirs. Add sifted dry ingredients and lemon rind alternately with milk. Rub sides of shallow baking dish with Crisco. Fill bottom with peeled and quartered peaches. Sprinkle with sugar and lemon juice. Pour batter over peaches. Bake in 350° oven about 30 minutes. Remove from oven; cover with meringue. (See recipe below.)

MERINGUE

2 egg whites
1/4 cup powdered sugar
Whipping cream, as desired

Use whites from the eggs in Hattie's Delight. Beat and slowly add the powdered sugar. Brown meringue in 325° oven about 15 minutes. Serve warm, plain, or with whipped cream as preferred.   Johanna Blazina

APPLE STRUDEL

5-1/2 cups flour
1 teaspoon salt
1 egg
2 tablespoons Wesson oil
1-1/2 cups lukewarm water

4 pounds green apples
2 squares butter
1 or more cups sugar, if apples are sour
1 tablespoon cinnamon

Place 4 cups of the flour in a bowl; add salt, egg and oil; stir with a fork, adding lukewarm water a bit at a time until it gets too thick to stir easily; then knead it as you add the remaining flour little by little until all is used up. Knead at least 1/2 hour, as the more you knead it, the more pliable the dough becomes. Add more flour, if needed, until the dough cannot take up any more flour and is soft and firm. Make into a ball, grease and place in a warm place until dough is warmed through. While dough is warming, grate the green apples including skin. When dough is warm enough, place a clean cloth on the table and work the soft, warm dough into a flat shape and stretch it gently by hand until it is paper thin. A rolling pin can be used, but roll gently. Chip off small pieces of butter on top of dough. Squeeze the apples to get out juice and spread the apples on the dough. Sprinkle sugar and cinnamon over the apples; if new green apples are used, add more sugar. Trim thick edges of dough and roll the filled dough jelly-roll style. Place in a greased 10"x16" baking pan and bake in oven at 325° for 1 hour or until golden brown. Serve warm. Apple strudel may be reheated and may be served with whipped cream, if desired.

Ika Yurkovich

EGG NOG PIE

1 cup milk
1 package instant vanilla pudding
1-1/2 teaspoons rum flavoring
1 cup whipping cream

Make a pie shell first and let it cool or use graham cracker crust. Whip the cream until stiff and refrigerate. Combine the pudding, milk and flavoring; beat until consistency of whipped cream, but do not overbeat. Combine with whipped cream, folding method. Pour into a pie crust and refrigerate for 2 to 3 hours. Sprinkle the top of pie with nutmeg.

Florence Knight, La Mesa, California

SPECIALTIES

CORN MEAL CREAM PUFFS

1 cup hot water
1/2 cup butter or margarine
1/4 teaspoon salt
1/2 cup yellow corn meal
3/4 cup flour, sifted
4 eggs

Combine hot water, margarine and salt in a heavy sauce pan and bring to a boil. Sift yellow corn meal and flour together and add all at once to boiling water. Stir vigorously over low heat for 2 minutes or until batter leaves side of pan and looks like mashed potatoes. Cool slightly. Add eggs one at a time, beating well after each. Beat 1 minute after last egg. This can be done by electric mixer—saves the old arm! Drop on ungreased baking sheet 2" apart. About 8 to 10 portions. Bake at 450° for 15 minutes. Reduce heat to 350° for 35 minutes longer. Cool. Cut slice near top. Fill with creamed ham, creamed chicken or ham or chicken salad. Excellent for luncheon with tossed green salad and a light dessert. (Recipe from Rose Hise Restaurant of Bodie, 1932)

Bettye Matson

"In 1932 copper prices fell to an all time low--five cents a pound, and Jerome started its decline."

CORN RELISH

1 dozen ears corn
2 onions, large
2 tablespoons mustard
1 red sweet pepper
1 small head cabbage
2 large green peppers

1/2 teaspoon tumeric
1/4 cup flour
1-1/2 cups sugar
4 cups vinegar
1/4 cup salt

Cut corn off cobs. Chop peppers, cabbage and onions. Mix thoroughly. Heat 2 cups of the vinegar to boiling; add sugar, salt, mustard, flour and tumeric, which has been combined with the cold vinegar. Heat to boiling, stirring constantly until slightly thickened. Then add chopped vegetables and mix well. Cook slowly for 1/2 hour.

Zera E. Veazey, Cottonwood, Arizona

CORN RELISH

1 dozen ears of corn
1 dozen green peppers
3 red peppers
1 quart onions, minced
2 quarts vinegar
1 quart sugar

2 quarts ripe tomatoes, chopped
1 cup ripe cucumbers, seeded, peeled, chopped rather coarsely
1/2 cup salt
1 ounce each celery seed mustard seed
1/2 ounce tumeric seed

Chop all ingredients fine and mix together with the fresh corn cut from the cobs. Boil for 40 minutes and seal the relish in mason jars while hot.

Hazel B. Logan

MOCK SALMON SALAD

1 pint carrots, grated
1/2 cup mayonnaise
1/2 cup toasted crumbs
1 tablespoon lemon juice

3 eggs, hard cooked
1/4 teaspoon salt
1/2 teaspoon onion juice
1 cup celery, chopped

Wash and scrape carrots and grate with coarse grater. Chop the eggs and add bread crumbs and salt. Add lemon juice and celery chopped finely. Add other ingredients. Serve on lettuce leaf.   Donna King

ENGLISH STEAK PUDDING

3 pounds round steak, cut in small pieces
1 pound suet
4 onions, sliced
1/2 sifter of flour, or more
1 cup water

Grind suet through meat grinder; mix well with 1/2 sifter of flour or more and salt to taste. Make batter (not too thick) with water; let it stand 1 hour. Line granite bowl with batter; do not roll too thin. Add to this the round steak cut in small pieces. Put in layer of meat, then layer of onions, salt and pepper, until dish is full. Pour 1 cup of water over meat and cover with remaining suet pastry. Tie cloth over top and put in kettle with boiling water. Water must not come quite to top of bowl. Cover and let steam 4 hours. Serve hot. (Submitted by Beth Cary)
Gussie Mader

ROEUF FLAMBE FROM FRANCE

2 or 3 pounds rump or any other lean roasting cut
1 tablespoon butter
2 tablespoons brandy
1 pound tomatoes
1 pound onions
1 eggplant
Herbs to taste and seasoning (I prefer rosemary)
Garlic as preferred for a fine flavour

Melt the butter in a dutch oven or casserole. When at foaming point, put meat in casserole and slightly brown on all sides on low heat. Pour over it the brandy, light it, then put around the meat the tomatoes cut in half, the sliced onions and the eggplant, if desired. Add herbs and garlic as desired. Cover with a tight lid and cook very slowly for 3 to 4 hours. Take meat out of the casserole and keep warm. Sieve liquor through a fine sieve and serve puree with the meat.
Bettye Matson

"For more than fifty years two smelter stacks, averaging 400 feet, were prominent landmarks in the Verde Valley. Clemenceau stack was blasted down on June 22, 1947. The Clarkdale stack was toppled on July 31, 1962."

POELLA (CHICKEN-SEAFOOD-RICE DINNER)

2 pounds chicken thighs and breasts cut in half (approximate weight)
1/2 cup salad oil
4 cloves garlic, sliced very fine
2 cups green peppers, coarsely chopped
3 cups onions, chopped
1/4 cup parsley
3 teaspoons salt
1 tablespoon paprika
1 pound cooked shrimp or lobster
1 teaspoon saffron, crumbled
1 teaspoon dried oregano leaves
1/4 teaspoon pepper
1 jar (12 ounces) whole clams
1-1/2 cups raw regular white rice
1 can chicken broth

In Dutch oven slowly heat salad oil. In the oil, brown the chicken and remove. Add garlic, green pepper, onion and parsley to the oil, and stir until onion is tender but not brown. Stir in saffron, paprika, salt, oregano and pepper. Put chicken pieces in Dutch oven. Heat oven to 350°. Drain clam liquid into 1 quart measure. Add chicken broth to clam broth to make 3 cups, adding water if necessary. Pour into Dutch oven, cover and bring to boil over direct heat. Add rice, making sure it is in liquid. Bring to boil again. Bake 1 hour until rice is done. Add clams and shrimp or lobster; cover. Return to oven and bake 10 minutes.

Margaret Mason

CURRIED SHRIMP (OR PRAWNS) a la Elena FOR TWO

1 can Campbell's frozen shrimp soup
1 cup milk
1 tablespoon curry powder
1 package (8-ounce) frozen shrimp, or prawns
Fresh mushrooms, sliced
1/4 cup onions, chopped
1/4 cup celery, chopped
1/4 cup sour cream
1/3 cube butter

Combine the soup and milk to make a sauce. Saute onions and celery in butter and add curry powder. To this combination add sauce which has mushrooms in it. Then add the shrimp or prawns and simmer not more than 10 minutes. Add sour cream and simmer 5 more minutes. Serve on fluffy rice. Surround this main dish with following condiments: coconut, chopped nuts, cut cubes of tomatoes, chopped eggs, chutney, et cetera.

Mrs. Charles M. Coppedge

"The last car of ore trundled down the tracks at 5:30 p.m. May 13, 1953. Jerome was turned over to the ghosts."

SPAETZLE (GERMAN EGG NOODLES)

1 cup flour, sifted
1/2 cup water
1 egg
1/2 teaspoon salt

Add salt to flour; mix, then add egg and water. This may be hard to mix at first, but mixture will soon become a smooth batter. Drop 1/3 of the batter on a cutting board (with a handle). Flatten batter down with spatula to about 1/2-inch thick. Into the boiling water dip the spatula, then cut batter into strips about 1/2 the size of little finger and drop the strips into the boiling water. The spaetzle will quickly rise to the top of the water. Cook for about 10 minutes, then strain. Pour melted butter on top, then serve. This is a good substitute for potatoes or other noodles.
Liz Pecharich

BARBECUE SAUCE (FOR BEEF or HOT DOGS)

2 cans tomato sauce
1 cup catsup
3 tablespoons vinegar
3 tablespoons bottled smoke
1 clove garlic
3 tablespoons barbecue spices
Salt and pepper to taste

Cook all ingredients together slowly for 1 hour.
Ellen Vojnic

GRANNY GOOK SANDWICH SPREAD

1 pound cooked hamburger meat
1 pound cooked bacon
8 to 10 hard-boiled eggs
1 onion
5 stalks celery
1 medium size bell pepper

Grind all ingredients, adding salt, pepper and garlic powder to taste. Then add sandwich spread and mayonnaise or salad dressing to make it easy to spread.
Stephen Sharp

EGG DISH FOR FOUR

4 pieces of toast, buttered
4 eggs
Any cooked meat 1/2" thick, minced
Cream sauce, as desired (see recipe)

Cream sauce ingredients:
Cream and butter
Parsley
A little mustard

Boil the eggs enough so they can be peeled without breaking (not hard). Toast and butter slices of bread about 2-1/2 inches square. Spread on the bread the minced meat until it is about 1/2 inch thick. Put the eggs on top of the meat. Pour over this a thick cream sauce, using the above ingredients according to personal taste.

Mrs. Lewis W. Douglas.

REUBENS GRILLED SANDWICHES

Rye bread (without caraway seeds)
Slice of cheese (Swiss or cheddar)
Corned beef
Sauerkraut
Dill pickle, slice thin
Mustard, if desired

Butter outside of bread and grill until brown. Serve with beer.

Geraldine Thomas

SWEDISH FRUIT SOUP

1/2 cup dried prunes
1/2 cup dried apricots
1/2 cup raisins
1/4 cup currants
10 cups water
5 tablespoons sago (pearl) tapioca

1 stick cinnamon
1/2 cup sugar
1/8 teaspoon salt
1/2 lemon, sliced
2 tablespoons corn syrup

Add prunes, apricots, raisins and currants to cold water and soak overnight; in the morning, add sago and cinnamon. Bring to simmering point, cover tightly and simmer 1 hour. Add sugar, salt, lemon slices and corn syrup; simmer 1/2 hour longer. Serve very cold for appetizer or for dessert.

Anna Cram

BRODET (FISH SAUCE)

1 large onion, chopped
4 tablespoons olive oil
1 garlic, minced
2 tablespoons tomato sauce
1 teaspoon parsley, chopped

1-1/2 cups water
2 tablespoons vinegar
2 pounds fish, cut in large
   pieces, or
Canned tuna may be used

This recipe is given in memoriam to Rose Radetich. Brown onion and garlic in oil; add tomato sauce, liquid and seasoning. Let this simmer about 10 minutes; add parsley, vinegar and fish. Cook until fish is done. Pour this sauce over Polenta (See recipe below).

POLENTA (CORN MEAL)

3 cups water
1 teaspoon salt

1 cup yellow corn meal
1 cup cold water

Bring water and salt to boil; add corn meal and stir constantly. Cook about 30 minutes. Polenta should be thick. Serve with Brodet.

          Sally Radetich Kozeliski
           Gallup, N. M.

SKEWERED SHRIMP

Large cooked shrimp, as desired
Mandarin oranges, as desired
 Sauce Mixture:
1 cup mayonnaise
1 tablespoon tomato paste
1 teaspoon Worchestershire sauce
1 teaspoon prepared mustard

Skewer large cooked shrimp, alternating with sections of mandarin oranges. Dip in the sauce mixture and refrigerate till served. (This is a recipe from "First Fleet Favorites," Staff Wives Commander First Fleet, Navy U.S.A.   Marilyn H. Foster

"A young Mexican, pack master with a train
of 200 burros, hauled spring water into the
town for domestic use. Later he returned to
Mexico and became famous as Pancho Villa."

COFFEE PARFAIT

1/2 pound marshmallows, cut up
1 cup strong coffee
Pinch of salt
1 cup whipping cream

Melt marshmallows into hot coffee; let cool. Add whipped cream in a folding motion until blended. Put into individual goblets and refrigerate. Makes about 8 servings.

Grace Moore

SPOOK HALL CANDY

2 packages small caramel squares
2 tablespoons butter
1/2 cup nuts
1 cup Chinese noodles
1 teaspoon vanilla

Put caramels and butter in double boiler and stir until the caramels are melted. Remove from stove and stir in the nuts, Chinese noodles and the vanilla. Have strip of wax paper ready and spoon the mixture onto the wax paper in small spoonfuls to harden before placing them into a candy dish or box for storing. Makes a popular treat for anytime and especially for Hallowe'en and for gifts of candy.

Laura Williams

CHOCOLATE FUDGE MOM'S recipe

4-1/2 cups sugar
1/4 pound (1 cube) butter, or margarine
1 large can condensed milk

3 packages (6-ounce size) chocolate chips
1 large jar marshmallow creme
2 cups broken nuts

Mix, stir constantly 6 minutes and 30 seconds from the time it starts to boil. Remove from heat and stir in the chocolate chips until dissolved, then add marshmallow creme. Stir until dissolved, then add nuts. Pour into buttered dish.

Shirley Hamilton

GAZPACHO

1 large can tomato juice
4 medium tomatoes
2 medium cucumbers
1 green pepper
1 canned green chilies
3 tablespoons olive oil
3 tablespoons wine vinegar
2 teaspoons salt

Put in blender or chop fine. Serve cold.

E. Mary Johnson

YORKSHIRE PUDDING

1 cup all-purpose flour
1 teaspoon salt
1 tablespoon shortening

1 cup milk
2 eggs, well beaten
1/4 cup shortening melted
or roast drippings

Sift flour and salt into bowl; cut in shortening; cream well. Add milk and eggs and beat at high speed for 10 minutes. Chill thoroughly in refrigerator. When ready to serve, place empty popover or muffin tin in oven until very hot. Pour 1 teaspoon shortening in each. Fill half full of batter. Bake at 425° for 30 minutes. Yields 12.

Mary Hufnagel, Tucson, Arizona

YORKSHIRE PUDDING

1 cup flour
1 cup cold milk
2 cold eggs
1/4 cup roast beef drippings, hot
1/4 teaspoon salt, or to taste

Combine flour and milk with a wire whisk until smooth. Add eggs one at a time and whisk until blended after each egg. Refrigerate covered Coat 9x11-inch or slightly larger rectangular pan with drippings; pour in flour-milk mixture. Bake at 425 to 450° for 35 to 40 minutes; or until highly puffed and crispy. Serve Yorkshire pudding with roast beef.

Katherine Moore Michaelsen

SARMA - STUFFED CABBAGE ROLLS

2 large heads of cabbage
2-1/2 size can of sauerkraut
2 pounds ground round
1/2 pound bacon, ground up
1 medium onion, minced; and 2 cloves garlic, crushed
1/2 cup rice
1 tablespoon salt
1 teaspoon pepper
1 egg

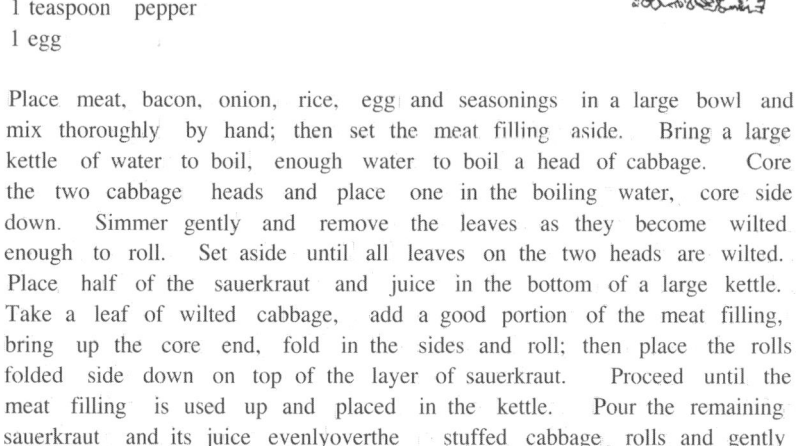

Place meat, bacon, onion, rice, egg and seasonings in a large bowl and mix thoroughly by hand; then set the meat filling aside. Bring a large kettle of water to boil, enough water to boil a head of cabbage. Core the two cabbage heads and place one in the boiling water, core side down. Simmer gently and remove the leaves as they become wilted enough to roll. Set aside until all leaves on the two heads are wilted. Place half of the sauerkraut and juice in the bottom of a large kettle. Take a leaf of wilted cabbage, add a good portion of the meat filling, bring up the core end, fold in the sides and roll; then place the rolls folded side down on top of the layer of sauerkraut. Proceed until the meat filling is used up and placed in the kettle. Pour the remaining sauerkraut and its juice evenly over the stuffed cabbage rolls and gently add enough cold water to cover 1 inch deep over the Sarma. Bring this kettleful to a simmer and cook gently for 1 hour longer. Note: The Sarma can be refrigerated and reheated as needed and it has an even fuller flavor after being kept overnight.   Ika Yurkovich

**HAVEN UNITED METHODIST CHURCH
IS NOW THE SOLE PUBLISHER OF
THIS COOKBOOK. ALL PROCEEDS ARE
USED TO BENEFIT THE CHURCH.**

**FOR MORE COPIES OF
THE COPPER TOWN COOKBOOK,
PLEASE CONTACT:
HAVEN UNITED METHODIST CHURCH
P.O. BOX 187
JEROME, AZ 86331**